Mastery of Anxiety and Panic for Adolescents

RENEWALS 458-4574
DATE DUE

Mastery of Anxiety and Panic for Adolescents

RIDING THE WAVE

Therapist Guide

Donna B. Pincus • Jill T. Ehrenreich • Sara G. Mattis

OXFORD
UNIVERSITY PRESS

2008

OXFORD
UNIVERSITY PRESS

Oxford University Press, Inc., publishes works that further
Oxford University's objective of excellence
in research, scholarship, and education.

Oxford   New York
Auckland   Cape Town   Dar es Salaam   Hong Kong   Karachi
Kuala Lumpur   Madrid   Melbourne   Mexico City   Nairobi
New Delhi   Shanghai   Taipei   Toronto

With offices in
Argentina   Austria   Brazil   Chile   Czech Republic   France   Greece
Guatemala   Hungary   Italy   Japan   Poland   Portugal   Singapore
South Korea   Switzerland   Thailand   Turkey   Ukraine   Vietnam

Published by Oxford University Press, Inc.
198 Madison Avenue, New York, New York 10016

www.oup.com

Oxford is a registered trademark of Oxford University Press

Library of Congress Cataloging-in-Publication Data
Pincus, Donna.
Mastery of anxiety and panic for adolescents : riding the wave : therapist
guide / Donna B. Pincus, Jill T. Ehrenreich, Sara G. Mattis.
p. ; cm. — (TreatmentsThatWork)
Includes bibliographical references.
ISBN 978–0–19–533580–4   1. Panic disorders—Treatment.   2. Anxiety
disorders—Treatment.   3. Cognitive therapy for teenagers.
I. Ehrenreich, Jill T.   II. Mattis, Sara Golden, 1968-   III. Title.
IV. Series: Treatments that work. [DNLM: 1. Anxiety Disorders—therapy.
2. Panic Disorder—therapy.   3. Adolescent Psychology—methods.
4. Adolescent.   5. Cognitive Therapy.   WM 172 P647 2008]
RC535.P56 2008
616.85′223—dc22

9 8 7 6 5 4 3 2 1

Printed in the United States of America
on acid-free paper

About Programs *ThatWork*™

Stunning developments in healthcare have taken place over the last several years, but many of our widely accepted interventions and strategies in mental health and behavioral medicine have been brought into question by research evidence as not only lacking benefit but perhaps inducing harm. Other strategies have been proven effective using the best current standards of evidence, resulting in broad-based recommendations to make these practices more available to the public. Several recent developments are behind this revolution. First, we have arrived at a much deeper understanding of pathology, both psychological and physical, which has led to the development of new, more precisely targeted interventions. Second, our increased understanding of developmental issues allows a finer matching of interventions to developmental levels. Third, our research methodologies have improved substantially, such that we have reduced threats to internal and external validity, making the outcomes more directly applicable to clinical situations. Fourth, governments around the world and healthcare systems and policymakers have decided that the quality of care should improve, that it should be evidence-based, and that it is in the public's interest to ensure that this happens (Barlow, 2004; Institute of Medicine, 2001).

Of course, the major stumbling block for clinicians everywhere is the accessibility of newly developed evidence-based psychological interventions. Workshops and books can go only so far in acquainting responsible and conscientious practitioners with the latest behavioral healthcare practices and their applicability to individual patients. This new series, Programs *ThatWork*™, is devoted to communicating these exciting new interventions to clinicians on the frontlines of practice.

The manuals and workbooks in this series contain step-by-step detailed procedures for assessing and treating specific problems and diagnoses. But this series also goes beyond the books and manuals by providing ancillary materials that will approximate the supervisory process in assisting practitioners in the implementation of these procedures in their practice.

In our emerging healthcare system, the growing consensus is that evidence-based practice offers the most responsible course of action for the mental health professional. All behavioral healthcare clinicians deeply desire to provide the best possible care for their patients. In this series, our aim is to close the dissemination and information gap and make that possible.

This therapist guide, and the companion workbook for patients, addresses the treatment of panic disorder and agoraphobia in adolescents. The onset of the disorder often occurs in adolescence and, left untreated, panic symptoms can continue into adulthood. Adolescence is a time of significant developmental growth, and therefore the impact of the disorder can be severe. Panic disorder and agoraphobia can interfere with school attendance, social functioning, and autonomous development. It has also been associated with higher rates of depression.

This guide uses a cognitive-behavioral therapy (CBT) approach based on the well-established MAP treatment program for adults. It has been specifically developed and tested for use with adolescents ages 12–17. Through psychoeducation, cognitive restructuring, and exposure techniques, adolescents learn about the nature of anxiety and panic and how to face their fears. An optional parent component involves parents in each session; handouts provide them with tips for parenting their anxious teen. The guide also offers suggestions on adapting the material for younger patients and for intensive treatment.

For therapists working with the adolescent population, this guide is a unique and valuable resource. It offers a proven and effective treatment that helps therapists work with adolescents to overcome their avoidance and deal with their panic.

David H. Barlow, Editor-in-Chief,
Programs *ThatWork*™
Boston, Massachusetts

References

Barlow, D. H. (2004). Psychological treatments. *American Psychologist, 59,* 869–878.

Institute of Medicine (2001). *Crossing the quality chasm: A new health system for the 21st century.* Washington, DC: National Academy Press.

Contents

Acknowledgments

This manual and companion workbook are the result of several years of work and contribution by many of our colleagues, including postdoctoral fellows and students. First and foremost, we would like to acknowledge the influence of previous work, manuals and workbooks on panic control treatment for adults by Dr. Michelle G. Craske and Dr. David H. Barlow. Their work served as a basis and foundation for the subsequent development of panic control treatment for adolescents. We would also like to highlight the contributions of Dr. Ronald M. Rapee, Susan A. Tracey, Dr. Emily Hoffman, Dr. Jamie Micco, Dr. Molly Choate-Summers, and Dr. Aleta Angelosante. We would also like to thank the many adolescents and families with whom we have worked throughout the years for their contributions to the development and evaluation of this manual.

Chapter 1 | *Introductory Information for Therapists*

Background Information and Purpose of This Program

This manual outlines a program based on the treatment identified as Panic Control Treatment for Adolescents (PCT-A), a developmentally sensitive adaptation of a cognitive-behavioral treatment of panic disorder (PD) with or without agoraphobia (PDA) for adults (see *Mastery of Your Anxiety and Panic, Fourth Edition* by Craske and Barlow, 2006). PCT-A is designed to be administered by therapists who are skilled in the conduct of cognitive-behavioral therapy (CBT) and exposure therapy for PDA. This treatment has been specifically designed for use with adolescent patients ages 12–17 exhibiting PDA (see Chapter 13 for using the treatment with younger ages) and has demonstrated efficacy in treating this adolescent population. This manual has been developed for the application of this treatment over 11 sessions. Each chapter provides extensive detail regarding the application of PCT-A treatment components, including strategies for dealing with a variety of patient responses to the delivery of these components. In addition, we are currently in the midst of evaluating PCT-A when presented in an intensive, 8-day format at our Center. (Please see Chapter 13 for an overview of how this treatment may be conducted using this more intensive format.)

Further, this manual contains an optional parent component designed to incorporate parents or caregivers more directly into the treatment of adolescent panic, given that many parents are unsure of how to approach the significant avoidance and distress that teens with PDA may exhibit. This parent component includes psychoeducation for parents as well as strategies for parenting anxious adolescents. See Chapter 3 for general instructions on carrying out this component. Parents are usually included at the end of every session. Moreover, at the end of certain sessions, therapists provide handouts to guide parental interventions related to specific treatment components. These handouts for parents can be photocopied from the appendix at the back of this book or multiple copies can be downloaded from the Treatments *That Work*™ Web site at www.oup.com/us/ttw.

Disorder or Problem Focus

Research indicates that PD not only occurs prior to adulthood, but that adolescence may be the initial peak period of onset (American Psychiatric Association, 1994). Studies investigating the prevalence of panic attacks in adolescents have reported that 35.9% to 63.3% of adolescents in community samples report panic attacks (Macaulay and Kleinknecht, 1989; King et al., 1993; King et al., 1996), while .5% to 5% report past or present symptoms sufficient to meet DSM criteria for PD (see DSM criteria listed below; Macaulay and Kleinknecht, 1989; Moreau and Follet, 1993; Hayward et al., 1997, 2000; Essau et al., 1999). Research on the prevalence of PD in a clinical population has indicated that between 2% and 10% of adolescents referred to outpatient anxiety and mood disorders clinics meet diagnostic criteria for PD (Last and Strauss, 1989; Diler et al., 2004), whereas between 10% and 15% of hospitalized adolescents received this diagnosis (Alessi, Robbins, and Dilsaver, 1987; Masi et al., 2000). Based on this research, current consensus in the field agrees that PD occurs in adolescence with a prevalence rate of approximately 1% (Lewinsohn et al., 1993). Modal age of onset occurs in mid-adolescence, typically after 14 years of age, with PD more common among adolescent females than males (Thyer et al., 1985; Kearney et al., 1997).

Diler and colleagues (2004) examined the clinical features of panic in 42 youngsters with a diagnosis of PD, in comparison to large samples of children and adolescents with other anxiety disorders ($n = 407$) and nonanxiety psychiatric disorders ($n = 1576$). Similar to the phenomenology of PD in adulthood, the most frequent and severe panic symptoms reported included palpitations, dizziness, chest pain, faintness, shortness of breath, and trembling or sweating. In another study examining panic in a clinical sample of 20 youngsters with PD and a matched-gender group of children and adolescents (aged 8–17) with nonpanic anxiety disorders, Kearney et al. (1997) found that avoidance plays an important role in the clinical picture, with 18 of the youngsters receiving diagnoses of PD also exhibiting agoraphobia. The settings most commonly avoided by this group included restaurants, crowds, school, small and large rooms, elevators, parks, and stores.

Comorbidity

PD is significantly associated with major depressive disorder (MDD) (Last and Strauss, 1989; Biederman et al., 1997; Essau et al., 1999). Essau and colleagues (1999) found that 80% of those in a community sample of adolescents with PDA also had MDD, whereas an additional 40% exhibited a dysthymic disorder. Diler et al. (2004) observed that adolescents with PDA exhibited MDD at significantly higher rates than those with nonanxiety psychiatric disorders (50% vs. 27%), although this frequency was not significantly greater than rates noted for youth with other types of anxiety disorder (44%). Other commonly co-occurring psychiatric disorders among those with PDA in this sample were generalized anxiety disorder (50%), separation anxiety disorder (21.4%), and bipolar disorder (19%) (Diler et al., 2004).

Prognosis

Evidence is accumulating that, if left untreated, the symptoms of PDA may span a chronic if fluctuating course throughout adulthood (Keller et al., 1994; Biederman et al., 1997; Wittchen, Reed, and Kessler, 1998; Yonkers et al., 1998). As noted previously, PD may place a child at high risk for concurrent depression, and depression in adolescence may have significant consequences for future functioning (Pine et al., 1998). Weissman and associates (1999) reported on impairments in adulthood among 73 individuals with MDD in adolescence, 10–15 years following initial adolescent assessment. In comparison to control participants without a history of psychiatric illness, those with adolescent-onset MDD evidenced a high incidence of suicide (7.7%) and a five-fold increased risk for first suicide attempt. Other researchers have also observed a link between adolescent depression and school failure (Fleming, Offord, and

Boyle, 1989), future marital dissatisfaction in women (Gotlib, Lewinsohn, and Seeley, 1998), and future substance abuse (Birmaher et al., 1996).

Diagnostic Criteria for Panic Disorder

The *DSM-IV-TR* criteria for PD is as follows:

A. Both 1 and 2:
   1. Recurrent unexpected panic attacks.
   2. At least one of the attacks has been followed by 1 month (or more) of one (or more) of the following:
      a. a persistent concern about having additional attacks;
      b. worrying about the implications of the attack or its consequences (e.g., losing control, having a heart attack, going crazy/insane);
      c. a significant change in behavior related to the attacks.

B. The panic attacks are not due to the direct physiological effects of a substance (e.g., a drug of abuse, a medication) or a general medical condition (e.g., hyperthyroidism).

C. The panic attacks are not better accounted for by another mental disorder, such as social phobia (e.g., occurring on exposure to feared social situations), specific phobia (e.g., on exposure to a specific phobic situation), obsessive-compulsive disorder (OCD) (e.g., on exposure to dirt, in someone with an obsession about contamination), posttraumatic stress disorder (PTSD) (e.g., in response to stimuli associated with a severe stressor), or separation anxiety disorder (e.g., in response to being away from home or close relatives).

Diagnostic Criteria for Agoraphobia

PD is divided into categories of with or without agoraphobia. The *DSM-IV-TR* criteria for agoraphobia is as follows:

A. Anxiety about being in places or situations from which escape might be difficult (or embarrassing) or in which help may not be available in the event of having an unexpected or situationally pre-disposed panic attack or panic-like symptoms. Agoraphobic fears typically involve characteristic clusters of situations that include being outside the home alone; being in a crowd or standing in a line; being on a bridge; and traveling in a bus, train, or automobile.

B. The situations are avoided (e.g., travel is restricted), or else are endured with marked distress or with anxiety about having a panic attack or panic-like symptoms, or require the presence of a companion.

C. The anxiety or phobic avoidance is not better accounted for by another mental disorder, such as social phobia (e.g., avoidance limited to social situations because of fear of embarrassment), specific phobia (e.g., avoidance limited to a single situation, such as elevators), OCD (e.g., avoidance of dirt, in someone with an obsession about contamination), PTSD (e.g., avoidance of stimuli associated with a severe stressor), or separation anxiety disorder (e.g., avoidance of leaving home or relatives).

Diagnostic Criteria for a Panic Attack

The diagnostic criteria for a panic attack include a discrete period of intense fear or discomfort in which four (or more) of the following symptoms develop abruptly and reach a peak within 10 minutes:

1. Heart palpitations, pounding heart, or accelerated heart rate

2. Sweating

3. Trembling or shaking

4. Sensations of shortness of breath or smothering

5. Feeling of choking

6. Chest pain or discomfort

7. Nausea or abdominal distress

8. Feeling dizzy, unsteady, lightheaded, or faint

9. Derealization (feelings of unreality) or depersonalization (being detached from oneself)

10. Fear of losing control or going insane

11. Fear of dying

12. Paresthesias (numbness or tingling sensations)

13. Chills or hot flushes

Development of This Treatment Program and Evidence Base

Relatively few studies have evaluated the effectiveness of treatments for PDA in adolescents. In an early study from our clinic, Barlow and Seidner (1983) treated three adolescents with agoraphobia and their mothers utilizing exposure-based approaches. Marked improvement was noted in two adolescents, accompanied by substantive improvements in parent–child relationships. A third was unchanged.

Ollendick (1995), in a multiple-baseline design analysis, combined elements of Panic Control Treatment, developed by Barlow and colleagues (Barlow et al., 1989) and procedures from Öst and colleagues (Öst et al., 1994). Participants were three girls and one boy, ranging in age from 13–17 years, and meeting *DSM-III-R* criteria for PD with agoraphobia. Treatment duration ranged from six to nine sessions, with termination contingent on panic-free status for 2 consecutive weeks. Treatment resulted in a decrease in the frequency of panic attacks for all participants, with the average number of attacks per week during baseline ranging from 1.5–2, and all participants achieving 2 consecutive panic-free weeks before termination of treatment. Improvement was also evidenced in reduction of agoraphobic avoidance and self-efficacy ratings in agoraphobic situations, changes that were maintained at 6-month follow-up. Based on these findings, Ollendick (1995) concluded that combined cognitive-behavioral procedures found to be efficacious in the treatment of PD in adults may be successfully applied to the treatment of adolescents.

To evaluate this proposition, we recently completed the first large-scale controlled treatment outcome study to evaluate the effectiveness of a developmental adaptation of Panic Control Treatment (Panic Control Treatment for Adolescents; PCT-A) for the treatment of PD (with or without agoraphobia) in adolescence under the direction of Sara Mattis, PI. The aims of this project were: (1) to evaluate the effectiveness of a developmental adaptation of PCT for the treatment of PD in adolescents as compared to wait-list treatment, (2) to determine the long-term impact of such treatment through follow-up assessment, and (3) to assess the impact of treatment on the quality of life of adolescents beyond the specific symptoms of PD. A total of 26 adolescents (aged 12–17) enrolled in the study; 24 completed the program and most follow-up assessments.

A 2 (Group: Control, Treatment) $\times$ 2 (Time: Pre, Post) repeated measures analysis was conducted on the clinician severity rating (CSR) from the ADIS-C/P and on the total score from each of the self-report measures. Analyses revealed significant Group $\times$ Time interactions for CSR ($p < .05$), and significant Group $\times$ Time interactions for the Children's Anxiety Sensitivity Index (CASI) ($p < .01$), the Multidimensional Anxiety Scale for Children (MASC) ($p < .01$), and the Children's Depression Inventory (CDI) ($p < .01$). Adolescents in the treatment group showed significantly greater improvement on these measures than did adolescents in the wait-list group. Additional repeated measures analyses were also conducted for the treatment group alone, including 3-month follow-up data. A significant main effect for Time was found for CSR ($p < .001$), CASI ($p < .001$), MASC ($p < .001$), and CDI ($p < .01$), as reflected in adolescents' improved scores on these measures from pretreatment to follow-up. Paired t-tests indicated significant differences between pretreatment and follow-up for CSR ($p < .001$), CASI ($p < .05$), RCMAS ($p < .01$), (MASC ($p < .05$), and CDI ($p < .05$). Means and standard deviations for all variables are presented in Tables 1.1 and 1.2.

Overall, this study provided support for the efficacy of a 12-week cognitive-behavioral treatment of PD tailored specifically for adolescents. The findings reveal a significant reduction in PD severity, as well as associated anxiety, anxiety sensitivity, and depression, among adolescents receiving PCT-A, relative to a control group. Notably, mean CSR remained in the clinical range for the control group, but fell to a subclin-

Table 1.1 Mean Clinical Severity Rating for Panic Disorder

	Control Group	Treatment Group
Pretreatment	5.41 (1.00)[a]	5.62 (.65)[a]
Posttreatment	4.75 (1.60)[a]	3.31 (1.36)[b]
3-Month Follow-up	——————	2.70 (1.75)[b]

Note: Means in each column with different superscripts differ significantly at $p < .001$.

ical range following subsequent treatment with PCT-A. Furthermore, analyses suggest that treatment gains were maintained at 3-month follow-up. These findings help provide a better understanding of the treatment of PD at its earliest stages. PCT-A was efficacious at reducing the symptoms of PD in adolescents, and also helped to reduce associated interference in adolescents' and families' daily lives.

Table 1.2 Mean Total Scores (Standard Deviations) on Self Report Measures

Treatment Group	Pretreatment	Posttreatment	Follow-up
MASC	65.85 (16.25)[a]	45.31 (22.75)[b]	47.27 (23.03)[b]
RCMAS	18.09 (5.19)[a]	9.62 (8.31)[b]	10.36 (7.87)[b]
CASI	40.00 (6.36)[a]	28.62 (6.55)[b]	30.27 (6.58)[b]
CDI	15.54 (7.63)[a]	8.77 (8.01)[b]	8.64 (6.97)[b]
Control Group	**Pretreatment**	**Posttreatment**	**Follow-up**
MASC	52.27 (23.53)[a]	51.25 (25.77)[a]	N/A
RCMAS	15.25 (3.95)[a]	10.75 (8.32)[a]	N/A
CASI	35.40 (7.29)[a]	32.67 (9.49)[a]	N/A
CDI	10.25 (7.68)[a]	11.18 (8.05)[a]	N/A

Note: Pre- and posttreatment means in each row with different superscripts differ significantly at $p < .05$.

CBT is a form of psychotherapy that fuses traditional behavioral components with cognitively oriented strategies. Although there are many variations in form, CBT is typically brief, problem-focused, and action-oriented, with an extant focus on altering behaviors and cognitions that may be acting to maintain current symptoms or problematic situations. In this regard, it may be contrasted with traditional forms of psychotherapy (e.g., psychodynamic treatments, etc.) that emphasize the generation of insight into causal variables that may have prompted current problems. Other common factors across CBT models include the use of techniques generated from basic learning and cognitive science principles; an emphasis on the interaction between feelings, thoughts, and behaviors; the use of homework to facilitate the generalization of skills; and empirical evaluation to examine the efficacy of specific CBT protocols (Antony, 2005).

One of the most common components of CBT protocols is the use of exposure therapy techniques, particularly in the treatment of anxiety- and fear-based disorders. Exposure therapy techniques operate on the assumption that through repeated interaction with an object, situation, person, sensation, or the like, negative emotions previously associated with that stimuli or situation, such as anxiety or fear, are eventually reduced. In more colloquial terms, by "facing one's fears" repeatedly, anxiety decreases in its intensity. Most researchers emphasize the process of *habituation* to feared stimuli as a main rationale for the effectiveness of exposure techniques, a process described further in Chapters 8 and 9 of this manual. Exposure therapy can be conducted in a number of ways and using a variety of associated techniques. Two common techniques used in exposure therapy with patients are "flooding" and "graduated exposure." The difference between these two techniques is the rate at which feared stimuli are presented to the patient, with the former strategy involving a relatively intense and thorough interaction with the most evocative fear triggers at the onset of treatment and the latter involving a slower progression toward highly evocative triggers, allowing for a great deal of practice at habituating to fear-evoking triggers prior to interaction with the most intense stimuli. PCT-A generally makes use of the more graduated approach to exposure, as described in more detail in the upcoming sections.

PCT-A is a developmental adaptation of Panic Control Treatment (Craske and Barlow, 2006), which incorporates interoceptive exposure (exposure to feared bodily sensations associated with panic), situational exposure, breathing retraining, psychoeducation, and cognitive restructuring over the course of 11 treatment sessions. PCT-A, similar to its adult counterpart, focuses on three aspects of panic attacks and related anxiety: the cognitive/misinterpretational aspect, the hyperventilatory response, and conditioned reactions to physical sensations (see Hoffman and Mattis, 2000). Initial sessions target the cognitive or misinterpretational aspect through psychoeducation in which the adolescent is given accurate information about the physical sensations of anxiety and panic and their relationship to the *fight-or-flight response*. Through such information, the adolescent learns that such sensations are harmless, and that a panic attack represents a fearful reaction to normal physical sensations. Adolescents are also taught strategies for identifying and challenging anxiety-provoking thoughts (e.g., "I might faint") by evaluating the evidence (e.g., "How many times have I actually fainted as a result of panic?") as well as their ability to cope (e.g., "Even if I did faint, would it be the end of the world or could I get through it?"). The role of hyperventilation in panic attacks is discussed, and adolescents are taught slow, diaphragmatic breathing to reduce the frequency and intensity of physical sensations that trigger and maintain panic. Conditioned reactions to physical sensations are addressed during the second half of treatment through interoceptive exposure that uses exercises and naturalistic activities to decondition fear reactions through gradual, repeated exposure to the physical sensations associated with panic. For instance, the adolescent is asked to breathe through a thin straw or to go running in order to elicit feelings of breathlessness. Through such exercises, the adolescent begins to separate physical sensations from an automatic reaction of fear, and to learn that such sensations are not truly dangerous. Finally, the adolescent develops a hierarchy of agoraphobic situations at the beginning of treatment, and situational exposure is incorporated as homework throughout treatment to encourage adolescents to approach situations associated with panic in their daily lives.

Risks and Benefits of This Treatment Program

Exposure-based treatments like PCT-A may be quite efficacious for the treatment of panic and other anxiety disorders. Following treatment, many patients report positive collateral changes to even non–anxiety-related symptoms and in other areas of functioning. Avoidance regarding important, previously feared situations may be reduced and, as a result, overall quality of life may be improved. However, this treatment does involve a substantial commitment to facing one's fears, and the motivation to both enter and tolerate feared situations may be difficult for some adolescents to contemplate. Those adolescents who are unable to enter into such a commitment willingly, because of difficult familial or environmental situations, severe comorbid disorders, or significant cognitive impairments, may not respond as positively to the use of exposure techniques or may express the feeling that such procedures are inconsistent with their wishes for treatment. This risk may be minimized through the use of thorough assessment, psychoeducation about treatment, and explicit discussion of the teen's commitment to persevere in this treatment at this time. Although initial studies indicate that this treatment has a very positive treatment response rate, as with any treatment, there is no way to guarantee success at the outset. Therefore, managing expectations for symptom remission, while maintaining adequate treatment motivation, may be a key therapeutic task.

The Role of Medications

Some adolescents may begin this treatment program under the care of a pediatrician, child psychiatrist, or other physician. Common medication treatments prescribed for PDA include benzodiazepines (e.g., Xanax® Klonopin®, etc.) and selective serotonin reuptake inhibitors (SSRIs; e.g., Paxil®, Zoloft®, etc.). Although some of these medications have evidence supporting their efficacy in the treatment of PDA, others have limited to no evidence to indicate their utility in reducing panic-like symptoms or related avoidance. When adolescents begin PCT-A on such medications, we generally recommend that they maintain a consistent medication type and dosage throughout PCT-A and attempt any subsequent reductions in medication level following treatment under the close monitoring of their physician, particularly in regard to SSRI treatment. Particularly when benzodiazepines are prescribed on a "PRN" or "as-needed" basis to the adolescent, we often work with the treating physician to reduce usage of these medications during the latter half of situational exposure sessions. This may be particularly important for adolescents who view benzodiazepines as a "safety signal" or a quick, albeit temporary solution to their distress, even in situations in which they now recognize that little to no danger will follow the physiological symptoms of panic.

Outline of This Treatment Program

Treatment Goals

The overall goals of PCT-A are to reduce three aspects of PDA that serve to maintain the disorder: (1) irrational, anxiety-provoking thoughts about the implications or possible consequences of panic attacks or their associated sensations; (2) conditioned fear reactions, especially to panic-like sensations; and (3) the use of avoidance and safety behaviors due to concerns about panic attacks or related sensations.

Irrational anxiety-provoking thoughts about panic and related sensations are addressed in two ways. First, the patient is given information about the functions and physiological bases of anxiety and fear and the bodily changes these cause. The purpose of this is to provide credible, nonthreatening explanations for the sensations experienced during anxiety and panic. Second, the patient is taught specific techniques for identifying and countering unrealistic thoughts about the likelihood and consequences of feared catastrophic events related to panic.

Conditioned fear reactions are addressed as follows. First, the concept of fear conditioning is explained. Then, patients are taught to identify bodily sensations to which fear has become conditioned by conducting sensation-induction experiments. Finally, fear conditioning is overwritten through intensive in vivo exposure practices, during which interoceptive and situational cues are combined. These are done initially with therapist accompaniment. Adolescents are strongly encouraged to accomplish the tasks and to enter the situations they have been previously avoiding. The use of avoidance and safety behaviors is addressed through education, as well as through the identification and elimination of all such behaviors.

Unique Features of PCT-A

Some of the distinguishing features of PCT-A include the following:

1. PCT-A combines elements of CBT (education, cognitive restructuring, symptom induction) with therapist-accompanied, massed interoceptive, and situational exposure. Skills are taught in a self-study format, with the therapist teaching skills during sessions and reviewing and practicing skills with adolescents.

2. It is highly intensive, being conducted in its entirety over a period of 12 weeks (or, as an alternative, 8 consecutive days, on 2 of which patients are working on their own; see Chapter 13). Every effort is made to get patients to the top of their fear hierarchies during situational exposures. Therefore, the time commitment for some individual exposure sessions may be greater than that typically experienced by patients and clinicians, depending on the nature of the exposure needed and the availability of local resources to conduct such exposures.

3. The primary focus of treatment, even during exposure, is on the frightening somatic manifestations of anxiety and fear.

4. In contrast to therapies that teach management of fear and related somatic symptoms, or use exposure manipulations staying in the present to limit distress, few arousal reduction procedures (such as slow breathing) are taught, and their use during treatment is generally proscribed. Arousal reduction procedures, including breathing manipulations, are treated in the same way as all other avoidance and safety behaviors. That is, their disadvantages are pointed out, and patients are instructed not to use them during exposure procedures.

5. Similarly, patients are encouraged to accept risk and uncertainty. For example, the search for triggers of panic attacks as a means of making them more predictable or avoidable, which is common in conventional CBT, is de-emphasized in favor of stressing that, whether or not triggers are apparent, all fear reactions (including panic attacks) are essentially the same and involve the same physiological processes.

6. Finally, the skills that therapists must have to work with patients in this treatment are different from those needed for conventional CBT or graded exposure therapies. For example, considerable effort must be made to motivate patients to provoke their worst fear, give up safety behaviors, and surrender to their emotions. Therapists must learn to judge when to push patients and when to withdraw. They must deal compassionately with dependency, refusal, and anger. And they must resist the urge to relieve patients' evident distress. Patients and therapists develop strong emotional attachments during treatment, which must not be allowed to detract from the goals.

Table 1.3 Outline of Sessions

Session Number(s)	Treatment Component
1–2	Psychoeducation (including nature of anxiety, model of panic attacks, fight-or-flight response, and physiology of hyperventilation)
3–4	CBT (including identifying cognitive errors such as catastrophic thinking and probability overestimation, monitoring thoughts, and cognitive restructuring)
5	Interoceptive exposure (series of symptom induction exercises)
6–10	Intensive exposure with initial therapist accompaniment (includes use of Fear and Avoidance Hierarchy, elimination of safety behaviors, and homework exposures)
11	Skill consolidation and relapse prevention

Session Frequency and Duration

This treatment is administered in 11 sessions and ideally completed over a 12-week period. Sessions have been designed for a duration of 50–60 minutes, but therapists should allow for flexibility. The exposure sessions in particular may require more time, as noted earlier.

Use of the Workbook

This treatment is designed to be administered in conjunction with the companion workbook for adolescents, which is an essential part of therapy. The workbook contains all of the didactic material to be presented during the course of therapy as well as exercises intended to facilitate application of the material or illustrate specific points. In addition, "quizzes" or study aids have been created for each chapter. Depending on the needs of the patient, these can be provided along with the chapter assignments to help guide their reading of the material or used as a quiz at the beginning of a session to "test" their knowledge of material from the previous session. For patients who need additional incentive to complete their readings, points can be earned for correct answers on the quizzes, and those points can be exchanged for a reward at the end of treatment.

It is important that patients bring the workbook to all sessions, along with their completed homework exercises.

Chapter 2 | *Assessment*

The Challenge of Assessing Adolescents with PDA

The adolescent years are characterized by a rapid rate of developmental change. For both parents and therapists alike, discriminating the normal processes of adolescent emotional development and social adjustment from a potentially concerning psychological disorder like panic disorder with or without agoraphobia (PDA) is a challenge. Although outright symptoms of PDA certainly represent a departure from the normal developmental trajectory of adolescent emotional development, and is one that clinicians typically recognize as potentially interfering, it is only through detailed assessment of an adolescent's medical, developmental, and psychological history; current symptom presentation; and functional impairment that accurate diagnosis may be assured.

Differential Diagnosis

In this chapter, we briefly detail the components of an assessment package that may be used to accurately identify PDA and other psychological disorders (e.g., depression, other anxiety disorders, bipolar disorder, etc.) that may co-occur with or need to be differentiated from panic symptoms. In Chapter 1, we reviewed the diagnostic criteria for panic disorder (PD), as well as briefly differentiated it from other anxiety disorders (e.g., specific phobias, social phobia, etc.) in which situationally bound panic attacks may occur. Nonetheless, it is important to also review this information in the *Diagnostic and Statistical Manual of Mental Disorders, Fourth Edition-Text Revision* (DSM-IV-TR; American Psychiatric Association, 2000) before assessment begins, in order to accurately identify any differential diagnosis issues that might arise (e.g., identifying the presence of recurrent, *unexpected* panic attacks in panic disorder vs. those triggered by the presence of a phobic object or situation in phobic disorders) during the course of an adolescent's assessment.

Types of Assessment and Time Commitment

This discussion focuses primarily on questionnaire- and interview-based measures of current symptom presentation and related impairment. However, since one target of this treatment is decreasing overreactions to physiological symptoms, we also strongly recommend that therapists take a thorough history of the adolescent's developmental and medical concerns or request such records from the adolescent's physician before beginning treatment, to identify any conditions that may be impacting their current presentation. Copies of any previous psychoeducational or neuropsychological testing may also be helpful for identifying any cognitive or learning issues that may impact the efficacy of cognitive-behavioral treatment for the adolescent, if these are suspected.

Once this information is secured, the therapist will then have choices to make about the length of the assessment battery to be given and the number of informants included in the assessment process. This assessment process may be as brief as 1 hour, or as lengthy as 4 or more hours, depending on the measures selected and the thoroughness with which they are administered. Although it is understood that third-party repayment for assessment services is a challenge to undertaking a lengthy assessment battery, it is vital to conduct some form of diagnostic interview, to collect at least enough information to discern whether the client meets current DSM-IV-TR criteria for PDA and to assure that any co-existing conditions, such as mood, disruptive behavior, or eating disorders, are not of a severity or interference level that would suggest they be the primary focus of treatment instead of panic symptoms.

Multi-Informant Assessment

Wherever possible, getting symptom information from multiple informants (typically the adolescent, plus at least one parent or guardian, and a representative teacher, former clinicians, or physicians, when possible) aids in creating the fullest picture of current functioning possible. In our experience, it is quite common for parents and adolescents to disagree about the nature and severity of presenting complaints and PDA symptoms. Involving additional informants, even through informal phone interviews, becomes of paramount concern when such parent and adolescent disagreements are particularly strong or when panic-related interference is observed most commonly by someone outside the immediate family (e.g., school nurse, guidance counselor).

Questionnaire-Format Measures

A number of self- and parent-report questionnaires have been designed to assess general domains of adolescent psychological functioning, such as anxiety, behavior problems, and depression. With the one exception noted below, none of these measures is meant to serve as a sole basis for the diagnosis of PDA and should not be used in place of diagnostic interviews, but rather only to augment the information collected during such interviews or other forms of assessment. Table 2.1 provides a brief list of some recommended questionnaires that may be helpful in assessing general psychological functioning during assessment.

One measure specifically developed for the assessment of PDA symptoms is the Panic Disorder Severity Scale (PDSS) (Shear et al., 1997). The PDSS was originally developed for use in the two, large-scale randomized control trials of the adult version of this treatment, most recently detailed in *Mastery of Your Anxiety and Panic, Fourth Edition* (Craske & Barlow, 2006). This measure has been adapted for use with an adolescent population into the Panic Disorder Severity Scale for Adolescents (PDSS-A) and is presented here as a brief method for assessing the severity, frequency, and interference of PDA symptoms among adolescents. The PDSS is a seven-item scale that provides ratings of several core features of PDA (panic frequency, distress during panic, anticipatory anxiety, panic-related avoidance of situations and sensations) and the degree of work and social impairment/interference due to the disorder. It has been shown to have good inter-rater and concurrent validities. The PDSS-A is identical to the PDSS except for minor modifications to reflect age differences (e.g., rewording degree of work and social impairment to degree of interference in school and social activities) and may be completed by

Table 2.1 Brief Description of Selected Self Report Measures

Name	Year	Purpose/Relevant Scales	Child/Parent Report
Revised Children's Manifest Anxiety Scale (RCMAS)	1978	Assesses the level and nature of anxiety in children/adolescents (6–19). Four scales: Physiological Anxiety, Worry/Over Sensitivity, Social Concerns/Concentration, and the Lie Scale	Child Report
Revised Child Anxiety and Depression Scale (RCADS)	2000	Assesses DSM-IV anxiety and depression diagnoses in children and adolescents. Six scales: SAD, GAD, Social Phobia, MDD, Panic Disorder, and OCD	Child Report
Multidimensional Anxiety Scale for Children (MASC)	1997	Assesses various anxiety dimensions in children. Four scales: Physical Symptoms, Harm Avoidance, Social Anxiety, and Separation/Panic	Child and Parent Reports
Childhood Anxiety Sensitivity Index (CASI)	1991	A modified version of the adult Anxiety Sensitivity Index. Measures anxiety sensitivity in children and adolescents.	Child Report
Children's Depression	1977	Measures depression in children and adolescents Inventory (CDI) aged 7–17.	Child Report
Children's Depression Inventory: Parent Version (CDI:P)		Parent report of depression in children, useful for early identification of symptoms and treatment effectiveness.	Parent Report
Child Behavior Checklist (CBCL)	1983	Assesses a broad range of children's behavioral and emotional functioning. Two broad scales: Internalizing and Externalizing.	Parent Report

the adolescent or parent with minimal rewording of items. The PDSS has been shown to have good inter-rater reliability and good concurrent validity, and has become the gold standard for assessing treatment outcome in PDA (Barlow et al., 2000). A copy of the PDSS-A is provided in an appendix at the back of this book.

Diagnostic Interviews

Although the PDSS-A allows for a brief, reliable screening and on-going assessment tool for PDA, we strongly recommend the use of diagnostic interviews to produce the most accurate and thorough representation of the adolescent's current functioning possible. Although it is possible to conduct an excellent and thorough, unstructured diagnostic interview, we recommend using one of several reliable and valid semistructured interviews currently available for the assessment of child and adolescent psychopathology, if time constraints allow.

Although several excellent semistructured interviews are available, in our research and clinical work we use the Anxiety Disorders Interview Schedule for the DSM-IV, Child and Parent Versions (ADIS-IV-C/P; Silverman & Albano, 1997) as a diagnostic interviewing tool. The ADIS-IV-C/P is a downward extension of the Anxiety Disorders Interview Schedule for DSM-IV (ADIS-IV; Brown, DiNardo, & Barlow, 1994). These interviews permit the diagnosis of all DSM-IV anxiety disorders, mood disorders, and externalizing disorders of childhood, and also provide screening questions for selected other disorders (e.g., psychotic disorders, eating disorders, and somatization disorders). The ADIS-IV-C/P uses visual prompts in the form of thermometers to obtain child ratings of fear, worry, distress/interference, and occurrence of physical sensations. Parents and children are asked to provide ratings, ranging from 0–8, of the child's fear and avoidance of various situations, and of the degree of interference the disorder has in the child's life. In addition to diagnostic information, the ADIS-IV-C/P provides a 0–8 clinical severity rating (ADIS-CSR), based on the degree of distress and functional interference caused by the disorder, and assesses fear and avoidance of 19 situations that adolescents with PDA commonly avoid.

Patient Self-Assessment

The workbook also includes materials for patient self-assessment, including the PDSS-A. The patient should read Chapter 1: Getting Started and complete the assessment material before the first session. At the beginning of Session 1, the therapist will review the pretreatment assessment material with the patient.

Chapter 3 | *Involving Parents*

Importance of Parental Involvement

Research on the importance of including parents in child and adolescent anxiety treatment has grown substantially during the past decade. Numerous studies indicate that children and adolescents have the most significant and lasting gains in anxiety treatment when parents are involved. Recent systematic research has suggested that incorporating parents more centrally into the treatment of children and adolescents with anxiety disorders may enhance treatment effectiveness and maintenance (Ginsburg, Silverman, & Kurtines, 1995; Dadds, Heard, & Rapee, 1992). Ollendick and King (1998) highlight the need for intensive parental involvement when treating children with fears and anxiety. They suggest that parents might be regarded as co-therapists, responsible for the implementation of procedures developed by the therapist and for giving children or adolescents ample praise and positive reinforcement for brave behavior. Although this may seem common-sense, a review of the literature reveals that involving parents directly in the treatment process has been the exception rather than the rule (Braswell, 1991). Although parents are often given independent instruction in the use of contingency management procedures (see Barrios & O'Dell, 1989; Braswell, 1991), actual involvement in the treatment process has occurred only in a limited number of studies. Since the parent is one of the most significant persons in an adolescent's life, and an adolescent's avoidance of activities often causes considerable disruption in most families, the inclusion of parents in the active treatment process should yield greater clinical benefit.

This guide includes session-specific instructions for the optional parent component at the end of each chapter. An appendix at the back of the book provides Parent Handouts to be discussed during certain sessions. You may photocopy the handouts from the appendix or download multiple copies from the Treatments *ThatWork*™ Web site at www.oup .com/us/ttw.

General Tips for Parental Involvement

As an adolescent is learning new concepts and tools for dealing with his panic attacks, it is very helpful to have parents on the "same page" as their child. This can be accomplished by teaching both the adolescent and his parents a "common language" regarding the most appropriate tools to use during a panic attack. For example, during a panic attack, a parent might suggest that the adolescent "restructure his maladaptive panic thoughts" or "notice the triggers of panic attacks" and "not avoid the feelings." While it is important for an adolescent to know how to cope most effectively with a panic attack, it is also crucial that parents also understand how to help most effectively. Thus, including parents in a portion of treatment sessions ensures that they will be able to help reinforce concepts that the adolescent learned in therapy.

Many parents of adolescents with panic disorder (PD) are worried that their child might be in significant distress during a panic attack, and may inadvertently reinforce the child's avoidance of places or situations that might trigger panic. It is important that parents are educated about the nature of anxiety and panic, the fact that anxiety won't hurt or harm their child, and the importance of nonavoidance of physical sensations and of situations that might trigger panic attacks. Although parents are typically given handouts and reading materials regarding the nature of anxiety and panic, it is also helpful to have parents join part of the session, to teach these important concepts in person.

A common fear of parents of adolescents with panic is whether getting rid of their adolescent's PD will make them feel "less close" to their child. Parents state that, unlike many adolescents who are trying to separate from their parents, their teenager tries to "stay close" to them out of fear of getting a panic attack and having to deal with it alone. This often makes parents feel a sense of importance and emotional closeness to their teenager. When attempting to treat the PD, it is important to discuss with the adolescent and his parents other ways that they might maintain a close relationship if panic attacks were no longer occurring.

Although parents can be involved in treatment in many ways, it is important to first discuss the plan with the adolescent and parent(s), so that both parties are comfortable and aware of the plan. In addition, the inclusion of parents at the end of sessions does not mean that they must be informed about everything the adolescent talked about in therapy; only the important treatment concepts need to be conveyed.

A Note About Flexibility

With any good treatment, some flexibility is expected, while still staying true to the concepts of the manual. If you plan to involve the family in treatment, parent(s) are typically invited in for the last 10–15 minutes or so of session. However, with younger or less mature teens, it is certainly possible to include parents throughout more of session (such as the last 30 minutes) if you think it is needed. However, while including parents, it is important not to lose rapport with the adolescent, who should always be the main focus of the session.

During the interoceptive exposure session (Session 5), it is helpful to have the adolescent choose which exercises his parent should perform right there in session. This helps the adolescent see that the feelings generated are uncomfortable for parents as well, and that these feelings habituate naturally even in people who do not have PD. In Session 11— when there will be much to discuss regarding plans for the future as well as debriefing, and the session may end up including the whole family for most of the time—try to leave some time for the teen alone in case there is anything he would like to say that he may not want to say with his parent(s) in the room.

A Note About Family Issues

This is not a family treatment, and you are not trying to treat the whole family. You are treating the teen while engaging the parents as co-therapists and coaches. While you should and will address parenting skills as they relate to the teen's panic, do not get embroiled in larger family issues, if possible. When these topics arise, remind parents that you have limited time to address their teen's panic and that is the reason for this treatment. Assure them that you will address some larger family issues if they are getting in the way of their child's progress, but that it is imperative to keep everyone focused on the goal of the treatment—helping the teen's PD. If necessary, you may also wish to offer assistance in finding referrals in their area for marital or family therapy after this treatment is over.

Dealing with Anxious Parents

Since anxious teens often have anxious parents, it can be helpful to have the parents practice the three-component model with their own anxious thoughts, situations, and behaviors. You may also have to highlight for them, when discussing parenting, how their modeling of anxious behaviors teaches their teen to act the same way. Discuss thoughtful parenting—parenting in such a way that they think to themselves "What did my teen just learn from that interaction/situation?" or "What message am I sending to my teen?" Refer to the handouts included in the appendix of this manual for more parenting advice.

Chapter 4

Session 1: Introduction to Treatment and the Three Component Model

(Corresponds to chapters 1 and 2 of the workbook)

Materials Needed

- My Cycle of Panic and Anxiety form
- My Goals form

Outline

- Review pretreatment assessment material
- Discuss the nature of anxiety
- Introduce the three components of anxiety
- Discuss the basic model of panic attacks
- Provide treatment overview
- Discuss the importance and benefits of practice and monitoring
- Set goals for treatment
- Assign homework
- Conduct optional parent component

Assessment Review

Review the description of the adolescent's panic and anxiety symptoms and associated behaviors from the pretreatment assessment material (see Chapter 2 of the guide and Chapter 1 of the workbook). As noted in

Chapter 2, panic disorder (PD) and associated symptoms may look similar to the symptoms of other anxiety and mood disorders; therefore, a pretreatment assessment meeting prior to session 1 is strongly encouraged. Whether or not the adolescent and her family have completed formal assessment procedures, be sure to address the following at the start of this first session:

- Frequency of panic (e.g., how many times per week or month does panic occur?)

- Situations in which panic is likely to occur or situations that are avoided due to panic

- Symptoms experienced during panic in physical (e.g., hyperventilation, perception of a rapid heart rate), cognitive (e.g., general fears/beliefs about panic, feared outcomes), and behavioral (e.g. avoidance or escape behaviors, over-reliance on safety figures) response domains. Focus on what kinds of panic symptoms are the worst.

Identifying Pattern of Adolescent's Panic

Identify specific antecedents of panic. These may include both internal and external triggers. Some adolescents may have difficulty with this, reporting that anxiety can occur at any time and that no systematic relationship exists between environmental situations or internal sensations and the occurrence of panic and anxiety. Try to help the adolescent identify internal cues that may trigger anxiety/panic (e.g., negative verbal cognitions, physical sensations, and catastrophic imagery). The following questions may be helpful for teaching the adolescent to identify antecedents:

- *What usually happens right before a panic attack?*

- *What is the first thing you feel in your body?*

- *What is the first thing you think in your head?*

- *What do you imagine might happen when you feel panicky?*

Begin teaching the adolescent to become an observer of his panic/anxiety versus a more passive participant in its occurrence. At the beginning of treatment, an adolescent with PD may feel some apprehension about intervening with his panic symptoms, or even helpless to make larger behavioral changes during highly emotional states. Encouraging an adolescent to take on the role of an "objective observer" during such states allows him to take a first step toward more adaptive behavior during the course of panic symptoms. This is often perceived by the adolescent as an acceptable and helpful method.

The Nature of Anxiety

Explain to the adolescent that fear and anxiety are natural, necessary, and harmless emotions. They are experienced by everyone and are part of the experience of being human. Discuss with the adolescent ways in which anxiety can be helpful (e.g., for athletes performing in competition, getting out of the street when about to be hit by a car). This can be introduced to the adolescent by saying:

> *You are here because we want to help you feel less scared and panicky. But tell me, would you feel scared if a car was driving straight toward you? Why would you feel scared? Might it be good to feel anxious or scared in that situation?*

Prompt for the answer that anxiety can help protect you from danger (i.e., it can help you get out of the way of an oncoming car). Explain that anxiety, however, is unhelpful when no danger is present or when the anxiety occurs too frequently or at a level of intensity that feels extremely uncomfortable.

Emphasize to the adolescent that fear and anxiety are reactions. Although he may not be immediately able to identify triggers, these triggers do exist and can be internal (thoughts, physical sensations) or external (particular situations). Explain to the teen that, given that these emotions are just one of many possible reactions to these triggers, it is possible to learn different ways of reacting that will help to reduce his levels of anxiety and panic over time. Since these feelings can also be helpful to the adolescent in genuinely dangerous situations, the goal of treatment is not to remove all fear and anxiety, but to reduce only the anxiety that is unhelpful or unnecessary. The following dialogue can be used to summarize:

When we talk about anxiety from now on, let's think of it as something we feel in response to physical feelings in our body, thoughts that we have, or situations we are in. We're going to help you learn to react in a more helpful manner to the anxious and panicky feelings you get. We still want to keep the anxiety you feel when a car comes at you, but help get rid of some of the anxiety you feel when you are not in real danger.

The Three Components of Anxiety

Viewing anxiety as global entity is not helpful. Inquiring if the adolescent finds it helpful if someone tells him to "just relax" or "stop being so anxious" may help illustrate this concept. A more helpful strategy, and one that provides cues for addressing anxiety more effectively, is to view it in terms of its components or parts and their interaction. Tell the adolescent that, in your work together, you are going to help him pay attention to the feelings, thoughts, and behaviors that are associated with anxiety. The first step for the adolescent is to notice what his body and brain are doing when he feels anxious. Use the Cycle of Panic and Anxiety in Figure 4.1 to visually illustrate the three components of anxiety (this figure can also be found in the workbook).

Physical Component (What You Feel)

The physical component of fear and anxiety consists of the bodily sensations that occur (i.e., feelings that happen in the body) during panic (e.g., racing heart, dizziness, sense of unreality, sweating, etc.). These sensations are part of an "alarm reaction" that is the body's natural response to fear and danger. You may want to use the following dialogue in your discussion:

The way you feel during panic is the way your body would naturally react if a car was speeding toward you or if you encountered a dangerous animal. During the next session, we will talk more about how

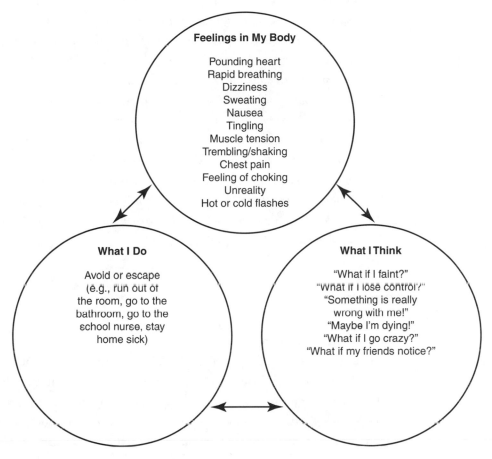

Figure 4.1
The Cycle of Panic and Anxiety

these sensations actually help you in situations that are really danger-
ous. A panic attack happens when the alarm reaction fires at times
when no real danger is present.

Cognitive Component (What You Think)

The cognitive component of anxiety consists of the thoughts and/or im-
ages that occur during panic (e.g., misinterpretations of bodily symptoms and their consequences). It is important to note that a person may
not be completely aware of an initial alarm reaction, even when in a
truly dangerous situation. The following illustration may be helpful:

For instance, if a car was speeding at you or a bear was chasing you, your attention would be focused on getting out of the way. You may not notice that your heart was pounding, you were feeling breathless, or that you were sweating, at least until the danger had passed. You would probably think these sensations were normal or to be expected in such a dangerous situation and not take any further notice of them. However, when the alarm reaction fires (i.e., when you have strong bodily sensations) and no real danger is present, because there is nothing dangerous to focus on "out there," your attention turns inward. This can lead to Panic Thoughts, which tend to be about losing control, being really embarrassed, or dying. Anyone who had thoughts like these and believed them would get scared!

Behavioral Component (What You Do)

The behavioral component of anxiety consists of the behaviors that occur during, or as a consequence, of panic. For instance, in situations in which panic has occurred, many people often try to immediately lessen or control their reactions by escaping or avoiding the situation. Unfortunately, these responses usually increase anxiety in the long term because they prevent a person from practicing, getting used to, and learning to handle the situation. To illustrate the concept of avoidance, use the following script:

Many kids find it more difficult to return to school after a vacation. One reason this can be so difficult is that kids get out of the habit of going to school, and school may seem a little more scary to them after a vacation. A similar reaction occurs when you avoid a situation because of panic. The situation becomes more frightening because you are out of practice and not used to handling the situation.

Interaction of Anxiety Components

The three components of anxiety may affect each other in a way that makes the panic and anxiety worse over time. Illustrate this by discussing the notion that the brain is like a watchdog that has been trained to be on the lookout for danger.

> When the watchdog notices anything that seems to signal danger, just like a real dog would, it sends a message to its owner—in this case, your body—which has been trained to listen carefully to the watchdog. So, when you go into a situation in which you had a panic attack, the watchdog perks up and says, "Something scary happened here before, I better be on the lookout to make sure nothing dangerous is around."

> Your body listens to the watchdog say that something dangerous could happen and responds by starting to prepare for this possibility. Your heart beats a little faster, your breathing speeds up, and so forth. However, the watchdog, who is looking very carefully for anything that might signal danger, notices that your heart is beating faster and interprets this as a signal that something scary might happen. He sends a message to your body that says "Oh no! The scary feelings are starting to happen again."

> The body then becomes more alarmed when it hears the watchdog say that something scary might happen, so it gets even more prepared by making the heart beat even faster, creating some adrenaline, and so forth. In this way, the mind and the body continue to play off each other in a sort of vicious cycle that leads to a panic attack. When these feelings continue, you may respond by having the urge to avoid or escape ("I need to get out of here!"). However, as we discussed earlier, these responses usually increase anxiety in the long-term because they prevent us from practicing, getting used to, and learning to handle the situation.

Explain to the adolescent that the importance of these components can vary across individuals and may vary within the same individual during different situations. For example, for one person, dizziness may be the prominent sensation, while for another, a racing heart may be important. Or, for the same person, experiencing a racing heart in a shopping mall may trigger fears of fainting and consequent embarrassment, whereas a racing heart in a deserted area may trigger fears of a heart attack without nearby help.

Complete a blank My Cycle of Panic and Anxiety form with the adolescent. Blank copies are provided in the workbook. Have him describe one or two panic attacks in the context of the three-part model. Identify his experiences in all three response modes, and pay particular attention to the interaction of components. Try to identify the trigger(s) of panic and anxiety.

Model of Panic Attacks

Although the three-component model helps give the adolescent a comprehensive overview of how PD can persist over time, he may still wish to better understand the physiology of panic attacks at this point. While this will be addressed more comprehensively in session 2, some key points may be communicated here.

Panic attacks are the result of a combination of a set of physical sensations (which may or may not be unexpected) and then a response of fear to the sensations. This fear further increases the intensity of sensations, which increases fear, and so on.

The frequency and occurrence of physical sensations can be due to:

- watching out for and scanning your body for physical sensations

- normal changes going on in your body that you notice more than most people because you are constantly keeping a watch on your body (e.g., digestion)

- tending to breathe a little too fast as a habit (subtle hyperventilation)

- stimulants (e.g., caffeine in soda) and activities (e.g., exercise) that increase sensations or awareness of them

A spontaneous (or "out of the blue") panic attack is also due to the occurrence of and attention to certain sensations, followed by a reaction of panic/fear of the sensations.

When people cannot find an obvious explanation for sensations, attention turns inward. People then try to make sense of what is happening and make faulty attributions about the experience (e.g., dying, losing control).

Treatment Rationale

Briefly reiterate the adolescent's initial panic attack symptoms. Emphasize that the factors that caused the first panic attack the adolescent ever had are different from those that still make him panic. His first panic attack likely occurred right after a time when he was feeling very stressed. People often get sensitized during such periods, which makes them more prone to future panic attacks. Now he has panic attacks because of the fear of the physical sensations he has when anxious (give examples relevant to the adolescent) and the ways in which his physical feelings, thoughts, and actions affect each other. Explain that this treatment will not focus on identifying the factors that caused the first panic, but will focus on identifying the factors involved in maintaining the panic.

Treatment Structure

Explain that, since anxiety and panic are reactions, the treatment teaches the adolescent new methods of dealing with these anxiety or panic responses. The adolescent's current methods (e.g., escape, distraction) may be effective in the short-term but only serve to increase fear of panic and ensure continued panic attacks in the future. Treatment will involve learning three strategies that are designed to target the three parts of anxiety (refer to the Cycle of Panic and Anxiety as you discuss these).

Cognitive (What You Think) will be addressed by teaching the adolescent to identify and challenge the assumptions and misinterpretations that serve to increase anxiety and provoke panic reactions. Challenging involves "becoming a detective"—treating thoughts as hypotheses, not facts, and examining evidence for them as well as evaluating the actual severity of predicted panic/anxiety consequences.

Physical (What You Feel) will be addressed by conducting exercises that help the adolescent become less fearful of the physical sensations of panic. The adolescent will systematically experience these sensations to change the automatic fear responses to non-fear responses. This will help the adolescent better recognize and cope with internal triggers that make panic attacks feel as though they are "coming out of the blue."

Behavioral (What You Do) will be addressed by changing the adolescent's tendency to escape or avoid physical sensations and certain situations. A list of situations that the adolescent avoids because of fear/anxiety will be created. Through exposure, the adolescent will learn how to face these situations gradually, but consistently, in order to overcome his avoidance.

Explain that changing the adolescent's panic response in one domain will have an effect on the other domains because of the interaction among the components (e.g., being less worried about dying when panic-stricken will diminish the intensity of the physical sensations and the strength of the urge to call for help). The goal is to "break the cycle" of panic through intervention with each of these individual treatment components.

Importance and Benefits of Practice and Monitoring

Practice

Treatment involves learning skills. Like any skill (e.g., learning to ride a bicycle) these skills must be practiced on a regular basis. Emphasize that the amount of practice that occurs between therapy sessions is directly related to how much the adolescent is likely to benefit from the treatment.

Monitoring

Monitoring allows the adolescent to become an expert at describing and understanding his panic and anxiety experiences. Explain that monitoring tools will be used as a stepping stone for each strategy learned during treatment and to see how he is doing throughout treatment.

The adolescent will use the Weekly Record to record the number of panic attacks as well as his levels of anxiety, depression, and pleasantness on a daily basis. Explain to the patient that depression often accompanies anxiety and that by treating anxiety, some adolescents find that their mood improves as well. By tracking his depression, as well as anxiety, together you will be able to simultaneously assess for such changes in mood. You will also be asking the patient to keep track of his level of pleasantness; this will help him become more aware of his positive affect and any increases that may occur throughout the treatment process. The two questions at the bottom of the form have to do with suicidal risk and provide an active, nonintrusive way for the adolescent to communicate any changes in suicidal ideation.

The patient will also record the details of each individual panic attack on the My Cycle of Anxiety and Panic form. Blank copies of both forms are provided in the workbook at the end of each chapter, as well as in an appendix.

Goals Exercise

Indicate to the adolescent that, now that you have reviewed the basic purpose of treatment and the types of feelings he will be working on, you will work together to clarify the expectations and goals he has for treatment. This exercise is meant to both assess the adolescent's motivation for treatment and ensure that treatment goals are appropriately tailored to the adolescent's personal goals. Have the adolescent complete the My Goals form in the workbook. Reinforce appropriate treatment goals regarding better awareness of panic symptoms and worry thoughts, along with reduced avoidance/escape behaviors.

Emphasize to the adolescent that treatment may not always be easy, as he will be asked to try new things to see if these new actions or ways of dealing with his feelings are more helpful. He may also gain some other very positive things by attempting these activities. For homework, the adolescent will complete the Weighing My Options form to identify any discrepancies between costs and benefits that may be a barrier to treatment.

After reviewing the adolescent's My Goals form, ask him if he is ready to make a commitment to these positive changes. If not, ask if he can make a commitment to trying activities in the next few sessions to see if they help, even a little bit. Emphasize that treatment will help him to deal with his panic feelings in a more constructive and helpful way.

Homework

✎ Have the adolescent review Chapter 2 of the workbook and complete the corresponding quiz.

✎ Instruct the adolescent to record the number of panic attacks and daily levels of anxiety, depression, and pleasantness on the Weekly Record.

✎ Have the adolescent complete a My Cycle of Panic and Anxiety form for each panic attack.

✎ Have the adolescent review the completed My Goals form.

✎ Have the adolescent complete the Weighing My Options form.

Optional Parent Component

Parent(s)/caregiver(s) join the adolescent for the final 10–15 minutes of the session. Use the following agenda:

1. Have the adolescent teach his parents (with therapist assistance as needed) about the following:
    a. Nature of anxiety, in particular, that it is a natural response to danger. The adolescent should explain to his parents that we don't want to get rid of helpful anxiety.
    b. Three Component Model/Cycle of Panic. The adolescent should be sure to use specifics from his own life (specific situations, responses, and physical symptoms).
    c. The adolescent's personal goals for treatment and how these may be accomplished using the treatment model.

2. Give parents a very brief, general overview of what to expect during the next 11 weeks of treatment, focusing on how each session

addresses a specific component. Emphasize that the therapist, parents, and adolescent are all on the same "team" and need to able to work together and from the same "playbook." Be prepared to answer parents' questions about the nature and course of treatment.

3. Briefly discuss and provide Parent Handout #1: Parenting Anxious Youth: 101, which addresses common parenting practices (overprotection, pushing too soon/too hard, etc.). Ask parents to review this over the next week.

4. Tell parents that they should also be completing the readings in the workbook. Parents and adolescent are encouraged to discuss material as they learn it and to complete workbook exercises together. If possible, the adolescent should take primary responsibility for these homework assignments, with parents monitoring and assuring their completion.

Chapter 5 | *Session 2: Physiology of Panic and Breathing Awareness*

(Corresponds to chapter 3 of the workbook)

Materials Needed

- No materials needed

Outline

- Review assigned reading and homework

- Discuss the physiological component of anxiety

- Conduct hyperventilation exercise

- Discuss physiology of hyperventilation

- Conduct slow breathing exercise (optional)

- Assign homework

- Conduct optional parent component

Homework Review

Review the adolescent's study of Chapter 2 of the workbook. Discuss her reaction to the treatment. Clarify any immediate questions that arise. Briefly review any homework (Weekly Record, My Cycle of Panic and Anxiety, and Weighing My Options forms). Discuss answers to the quiz, and address any questions that the adolescent answered incorrectly.

Physiological Component of Anxiety

This session focuses on the physiological component of anxiety. Begin by reminding the adolescent that the physical sensations of panic are physiological reactions when danger or threat is perceived. These sensations represent the activation of the fight-or-flight system (first presented in Chapter 2 of the workbook).

The activation of the fight-or-flight system causes reactions in many systems, all of which serve adaptive and protective purposes. Briefly review the physiological responses described here, focusing particularly on those symptoms that are relevant to the adolescent.

Cardiovascular (Heart)

The heart pumps faster and harder to get more blood and oxygen to parts of the body that will be used to fight or flee. This can be felt as the heart racing or beating very fast. Blood is also directed toward large muscle groups needed for running (such as thighs) or fighting (biceps). Thus, blood is redirected away from the skin and smaller muscles. This can have the effect of cold hands.

Respiratory (Breathing)

For more oxygen to be circulated, one must breathe faster and deeper. This can be felt as heavy breathing, pains and tightness in the chest and, in some instances, as feelings of breathlessness. In addition, since blood is being redirected toward large muscle groups, areas that are getting less blood are also getting less oxygen, although not enough to be dangerous. This can be felt as tingling or numbness in fingers, dizziness, and light-headedness.

Sweat Glands

Activation of the fight-or-flight system is hard work. Thus, sweating, which is the body's method of cooling down, occurs. This is also adaptive since it makes the skin more slippery and thus harder for a predator to hold on.

Miscellaneous

Pupils dilate to let in more light, which can result in blurred vision or spots in front of the eyes. Salivation decreases, which results in a dry mouth. Muscles tense up to prepare for action, which can create feelings of tension and muscle aches, as well as trembling.

Summary

Explain that the sensations of panic can last for some time because it takes a while for the chemicals involved, like adrenaline, to break down. This delay makes it easier for the fight-or-flight system to get reactivated, which is adaptive since, in nature, danger often returns. The fight-or-flight system is thought to be an "all or nothing" system (although a person may experience physiological arousal for some time without activating the system). Thus, it is likely that the patient will experience sensations in several areas at once. Elicit examples of different sensations the adolescent experiences.

Sensations may also be present and increasing before the fight-or-flight system actually becomes activated. Thus, the patient has the ability to intervene. However, there is probably a point-of-no-return at which a panic attack will happen. It is important to note that even when the system becomes activated, the individual can decrease the duration and intensity of the attack through application of behavioral strategies taught in this manual.

Discuss with the adolescent the relationship between panic sensations, normal physiology, and their survival value (covered in detail in Chapter 3 of the workbook). You can use the following script to convey the essential points:

> *The sensations of panic happen automatically in response to danger or threat, and protect us by facilitating the fight-or-flight response. The*

purpose of the sensations is to physically prepare the body for action (i.e., fighting or fleeing). In the times of our distant ancestors, who were mostly hunters and gatherers, it was very important that an automatic response took over that caused immediate action when there was danger. For example, when there was a vicious lion, our ancestors had to immediately attack or run in order not to be killed. Even today, this kind of automatic response is necessary, for example, when a car is speeding toward you.

Hyperventilation Exercise

To demonstrate the impact of physiological sensations on anxiety, conduct a hyperventilation (HV) exercise with the adolescent. Be sure not to provide the patient with too much preliminary information about the exercise. Simply tell her that you want to test something out to see how her body reacts.

Therapist Note

■ *The HV exercise can cause some patients, especially those who are particularly sensitive to breathing-related panic cues, to experience some anxiety. If this occurs, focus the patient on accurately monitoring her breathing and, to whatever degree possible, on her habituation to any fear of these symptoms, while they reduce naturally over time.* ■

Here are the steps to follow:

1. Briefly demonstrate the exercise for the patient. Take three or four deep breaths and exhale very hard at about three times the normal rate.

2. Have the patient stand up; instruct her to breathe very fast and very deeply (as if trying to blow up a balloon) until you tell her to stop (after 90 seconds).

3. Have the patient engage in the HV exercise. Be sure that she maintains an adequate speed and depth of breathing. You should do the exercise along with the adolescent for encouragement and modeling.

4. Continue the exercise for 90 seconds, unless the patient wants to stop earlier. If only a few seconds have elapsed, encourage the patient to try again.

5. At the conclusion of the HV exercise, have the patient sit down and breathe slowly until all symptoms have abated.

When the adolescent has recovered, inquire about the sensations experienced during the HV exercise. Specifically, ask the adolescent how similar each sensation was to her naturally occurring panic. Point out that the emotional aspects of the exercise may not have been similar to naturally occurring panic since she knows what is happening and may feel as if she is in a safe place, particularly if anxiety was low during the exercise. Be sure to comment on the importance and contribution of the cognitive component if no fear or anxiety was present during the HV exercise.

Physiology of Hyperventilation

Now that the HV exercise has been conducted, you should discuss the physiology of HV with the adolescent using the information provided in the following paragraphs.

Therapist Note

■ *If necessary, tailor the material to the patient's ability to understand. The main message to convey is that many people hyperventilate during anxiety and at other times, and that this can produce some of the symptoms of panic and anxiety. Furthermore, hyperventilation is not dangerous; as soon as it is discontinued, the body returns to its normal state and symptoms disappear.* ■

The purpose of breathing is to provide the body with oxygen and to get rid of carbon dioxide. While hyperventilation doesn't change the amount of oxygen in the body, it does cause a low level of carbon dioxide. This low level of carbon dioxide is not dangerous, but often causes disturbing physical sensations. During the hyperventilation or overbreathing exercise, the patient did not get more oxygen into her body, but she did get rid of more carbon dioxide than usual.

The purpose of the HV exercise was to demonstrate the similarity between an exercise that lowers carbon dioxide levels and the symptoms experienced during panic. It is important to remember that hyperventilation can occur in other ways that are not as dramatic or obvious as that observed during the HV exercise. For example, rapid, shallow breathing, frequent sighing, or frequent yawning results in low carbon dioxide levels in the body.

Stress that HV is not dangerous at all. All it means is that the body is getting rid of more carbon dioxide than usual. You may also want to briefly review some of the explanations for why low carbon dioxide produces physical sensations or symptoms. Discuss one or two of the following points, depending on their relevance for this particular adolescent:

■ The body gets the message to conserve oxygen by tightening the blood vessels. This produces heart palpitations and a racing heart, since the heart must pump faster and harder to compensate for the tightened vessels.

■ Less oxygen gets dropped off at tissues and cells. This can produce sensations like pins and needles, numbness, and cold/clammy hands.

■ Since blood vessels are tightening, less oxygen gets to the brain. Again, this is not enough to be dangerous, but enough to create symptoms such as dizziness, lightheadedness, feelings of faintness, confusion, unreality, and blurred vision.

■ The low carbon dioxide level sends a message to the breathing center in the brain to slow down breathing. However, whatever led to the HV may still be present, causing one to want to breathe faster. It is thought that this conflict may lead to symptoms such as breathlessness.

Point out again that a low level of carbon dioxide is harmless and that symptoms will disappear as soon as the HV is stopped and breathing is back to normal. Explain that HV can be part of the fight-or-flight response. Therefore, panic-related fear can become automatically associated with HV. Also, remind the adolescent that most HV is not as obvious as the HV exercise; people can hyperventilate without being aware of it.

Slow Breathing Exercise (optional)

To help the patient become more aware of her breathing patterns, you may want to conduct a slow breathing exercise. This exercise is optional, but may be helpful for adolescents who are very sensitive to breathing-related panic cues or who have a tendency to hyperventilate during panic attacks.

Begin with a discussion about overbreathing. Explain that emotions, such as stress and anxiety, can affect breathing rate and that many people with panic disorder tend to overbreathe during panic. In addition to overbreathing during panic, people with anxiety and panic tend to over-breathe frequently, resulting in chronically low levels of carbon dioxide. In this case, even small changes in the carbon dioxide level, caused by such things as a yawn or sigh, can produce sensations such as dizziness, heart palpitations, tingling, and the like. These sudden unexpected symptoms can trigger a panic attack that seems to come from "out of the blue," since the person does not feel like she is hyperventilating.

People who overbreathe also tend to use their chest muscles, instead of the abdominal muscles (diaphragm) for breathing. Since chest muscles were not meant for breathing, chest breathing can result in tired and tense chest muscles, chest tightness, and occasional chest pain.

Explain that breathing is normally under the body's automatic control. However, it is one of the few automatic processes in which people can exert voluntary control (e.g., during swimming, blowing up a balloon). By learning to change breathing patterns, a patient can decrease the frequency of sensations that may be triggering panic, as well as the intensity of sensations that occur during a panic attack.

Exercise Instructions (optional)

This exercise is designed to help the patient learn to slow her breathing. The patient should be able to breathe comfortably at the normal rate (10–14 breaths per minute) and be able to breathe even more slowly during anxiety/panic episodes.

To begin, teach the adolescent to breathe diaphragmatically or abdominally. First, demonstrate taking this kind of breath for the adolescent. Then have the adolescent practice by having her place one hand on her chest and the other hand on her stomach, just above the navel. This posture should ensure that respiration is coming from the diaphragm (i.e., only the lower hand should move). If the adolescent has difficulty, try using any of the following suggestions:

- *Imagine that there is a thin tube extending from your mouth to the bottom of your lungs. At the bottom of this tube is a bubble. Imagine breathing into this tube to fill the bubble.*

- *Forcefully push out your stomach before taking a breath. This will help expand the diaphragm and make room for air.*

- *Place a light book on your stomach. You should strive to push the book up and down while breathing.*

- *Lay on your stomach while on the floor or a bed. Your arms should be cradled under your head. This posture makes it very difficult to chest breathe.*

Once the adolescent has learned to breathe diaphragmatically, continue with the slow breathing exercise following these steps:

1. Have the patient relax for a few seconds before starting.

2. Do not have the patient do slow breathing yet. Tell the patient that she should breathe at her normal rate and depth. Each breath should be smooth and even.

3. Have the patient place one hand on her chest and one hand on her diaphragm.

4. As the patient inhales, count out loud at a rate that matches the patient's normal rate of breathing. Follow this order: "Inhale 1, 2, 3 . . . Exhale."

5. Continue the practice for about 1 minute.

6. Inquire about and respond to any problems or questions from the adolescent. Give feedback on her breathing if necessary.

7. Repeat the practice for an additional minute. The adolescent should count to herself during this practice. Give feedback if necessary.

Instructions for Home Practice (optional)

Tell the adolescent that initial practice sessions of the slow breathing exercise should be done in situations that are conducive to concentration and relaxation (e.g., in a quiet room, comfortable chair, etc.). Once the skill is learned, the practice sessions can be conducted in more challenging surroundings (e.g., while watching TV, standing in line, etc.). Emphasize that practice sessions should be done regularly because it helps the adolescent to develop the ability to use slow breathing effectively (i.e., to reduce the frequency and intensity of panic-related sensations).

Inform the patient that she may experience physical sensations when practicing the exercise (e.g., dizziness, breathlessness). Remind the adolescent where these sensations come from. Instruct her that if this happens and she is unable to tolerate these sensations, she may briefly stop the exercise (for a few seconds) until the symptoms reduce, and then begin again.

Homework

✎ Have the adolescent review Chapter 3 of the workbook and complete the corresponding quiz.

✎ Instruct the adolescent to record the number of panic attacks and daily levels of anxiety, depression, and pleasantness on the Weekly Record.

✎ Have the adolescent complete a My Cycle of Panic and Anxiety form for each panic attack.

✎ Have the adolescent practice slow breathing exercise (optional).

Parent(s)/caregiver(s) join the adolescent for the final 10–15 minutes of the session. Use the following agenda:

1. Have the adolescent teach her parents (with therapist assistance as needed) about the following:
   a. fight-or-flight response
   b. HV/overbreathing

2. Conduct the HV exercise with the parents.

3. Discuss and provide Parent Handout #2: Behavioral Principles for Parenting Anxious Youth, which addresses positive reinforcement, active ignoring, and labeled praise for adolescents.

4. Assign homework to the parents along with the adolescent. Parents and adolescent are encouraged to discuss material as they learn it and to complete workbook exercises together.

Chapter 6

Session 3: Cognitive Component of Anxiety: Probability Overestimation and Catastrophic Thinking

(Corresponds to chapter 4 of the workbook)

Materials Needed

- Thought Record

Outline

- Review assigned reading and homework

- Discuss the cognitive component of anxiety

- Introduce probability overestimation

- Introduce catastrophic thinking

- Practice monitoring anxiety/panic triggers and thoughts

- Assign homework

- Conduct optional parent component

Homework Review

Review the patient's study of Chapter 3 of the workbook. Discuss the adolescent's reaction to the treatment. Clarify any immediate questions that arise. Briefly review any homework (e.g., Weekly Record, My Cycle of Panic and Anxiety form). Discuss answers to the quiz and address any questions that the adolescent answered incorrectly.

The cognitive component of anxiety was introduced and briefly discussed in Session 1. In this session, you will provide the adolescent with more detail. Begin by explaining that anxiety/panic can have an effect on what we think. Like the physiological responses discussed in Session 2, this is also part of the fight-or-flight system that helps to protect us. When danger is noticed, attention automatically shifts onto the source of danger, and the individual scans his surroundings for anything that signals threat. This can interfere with concentration and memory, but is protective since it is more important to focus on possible danger than on the tasks at hand.

When no real danger or threat can be found, however, the search for danger is turned inward. The individual's thoughts then become occupied with predictions about the effects or consequences of anxiety (e.g., dying, losing control). He might think, "If nothing *out there* is making me feel anxious, there must be something wrong *inside* me." (Remind the adolescent of the concept of panic thoughts introduced in Session 1). This search can also interfere with concentration and memory.

Anticipating the possibility of future panic attacks leaves people feeling chronically tense and vigilant. This anxious apprehension fuels the panic cycle. To illustrate this, use the following examples:

> *Think of how you might feel if swimming at a beach where a shark had recently been seen. You would be constantly vigilant to any signs of possible danger. For example, minnows moving through the water or seaweed touching you would be interpreted as a possible shark, leading to increased anxiety. In contrast, if you were at a beach where no sharks had ever been seen, you would probably not even pay attention to the minnows or the seaweed, and you would feel much more relaxed. The shark is like the fear of a panic attack, which causes you to be constantly on the lookout for signs of danger.*

> *Or, think how it feels to be home alone, particularly after watching a scary movie. You might interpret small sounds (e.g., a bird or squirrel on the roof, creaks) in a scary way (e.g., "Someone's coming to get me!"). In other situations (e.g., during the day, when others are*

around, after watching a relaxing movie), you probably wouldn't even notice these sounds.

Finally, you can ask the adolescent how he feels in a haunted house, again illustrating the idea of being on the lookout for danger. These examples should help him understand the concepts of anxious apprehension and vigilance, and how they fuel the panic cycle.

Next you will introduce two cognitive errors that people with panic disorder (PD) commonly make: probability overestimation and catastrophic thinking.

Probability Overestimation

Probability overestimation is a cognitive error in which an individual predicts that an unlikely event is likely to happen (i.e., he overestimates the probability that an event will occur). Use the example of playing the lottery to illustrate probability overestimation.

> *A lot of people play the lottery because they overestimate their chances of winning. This may cause them to go out of their way to buy lottery tickets, sometimes traveling a far distance or standing in long lines if the jackpot is big. They may also plan what they'll do with the money "when they win."*

In the case of playing the lottery, probability overestimation may generate excitement about winning and then disappointment at losing. Explain to the patient that probability overestimations can also create or intensify anxiety/fear. Overestimating the chances of something bad happening causes a person unnecessary anxiety and panic. You may want to use the following example to illustrate:

> *For example, a teenager with panic might think to himself, "I am definitely going to feel sick and will panic at the school dance on Friday night, and I will probably throw up." That is an example of probability overestimation, because it is also very possible that he might go to the school dance and not feel sick or panic. In fact, there is also a good probability that he might have a good time. Also, if he stopped to think to himself, "Have I gone to school dances before and*

not felt sick or panicked?" The answer is probably yes. Therefore, we don't want to overestimate the chances that any of these situations will occur, because the likelihood of getting sick and throwing up and panicking at the dance is very small.

Explain to the patient that probability overestimations tend to occur repeatedly despite disconfirmation. There are three main reasons for this:

1. The person engaged in some protective behavior (i.e., escaped, called for help) that he feels prevented the dire consequences; thus, he believes that "it" could still happen.

2. The person attributes the nonoccurrence of the predicted consequence of panic to luck.

3. The person's thoughts about the situation have become automatically associated with feeling anxious.

You may want to use the following dialogue to present these points:

Even though people lose the lottery, they keep on playing, thinking that one day they will hit the jackpot. Likewise, even though nothing bad happened when you panicked the last time, you are still afraid of the next panic attack. You might think the only reason you avoided terrible consequences last time was because you had someone there to help you or you were able to leave the situation. Perhaps you think you have just been lucky and maybe next time your luck will run out. Or, you have felt anxious about the situation so many times that you automatically have scary thoughts about the situation.

Identifying Probability Overestimations

Demonstrate to the patient how to identify probability overestimations. Help him identify at least two of his probability overestimations related to panic (use the past week's monitoring forms for examples).

You can explain the model of anxiety using the metaphor of a buoy on the ocean. When the seas are rough, the buoy gets tossed around. When the seas are calm, the buoy simply floats. The interpretation of an event can move the buoy (i.e., emotion) into either rough or calm waters. Illustrate how predictions/cognitions can either increase or decrease anxiety from a neutral mid-point from one extreme (anxiety/panic) to the other extreme (relaxation). For example, if the adolescent interprets a racing heart as an impending heart attack, his emotion will be charged toward the panic end (moving the buoy into rough waters), which would further increase the heart racing. If he interprets the same sensation as just being nervous or even excited, then his emotion will be charged toward the relaxation end (moving the buoy into calm waters) and the racing heart will diminish.

Catastrophic Thinking (Thinking the Worst)

Another common cognitive error for people with PD is *catastrophic thinking*, or thinking that the worst thing imaginable is going to happen. The individual perceives the consequence of panic as "catastrophic," "intolerable," "dangerous," or "insufferable," when it actually is not. This kind of maladaptive cognition can increase anxiety and the frequency of panic attacks or panic-like sensations. Illustrate catastrophic thinking by giving examples of catastrophic thoughts:

- *If I faint, I may never regain consciousness.*

- *If other people noticed that I was having a panic attack, I could never face them again.*

- *If I have a panic attack at the dance on Friday night, it will be the worst thing in the world.*

- *If I have a panic attack, I may die.*

- *If I panic and then throw up, I'll lose all my friends and will wind up being lonely because people will think I am strange.*

Point out to the adolescent that if a "catastrophic" event were to happen, the occurrence is not as "catastrophic" as the patient imagines (e.g., fainting is an adaptive mechanism and the worst that can happen is a brief feeling of disorientation).

Identifying Catastrophic Thoughts

Demonstrate to the patient how to pursue catastrophic thoughts. Help the patient to identify at least two of his catastrophic thoughts related to panic.

Illustrate how these types of thoughts can create and/or intensify anxiety and panic-like sensations:

> *For example, sometimes when people have catastrophic thoughts, these thoughts can start the whole cycle of anxiety. If you think to yourself, "I will likely panic when I go to the dance Friday night," then this thought is likely to trigger some physical reactions in your body. As you walk into the dance, your heart may start to beat faster, your stomach might feel uneasy, and you might feel jittery. All of these physical feelings are getting stirred up to protect you, because you are thinking a thought that is scaring you. This is an example of how thoughts can actually generate panic-like sensations in your body.*

Therapist Note

> ■ *The patient can be told that probability overestimations and catastrophic thoughts are not necessarily mutually exclusive. Some cognitions may meet the criteria for both types of errors. That is, he may be overestimating the likelihood of an imagined catastrophe.* ■

Monitoring Triggers and Subsequent Cognitions

Tell the patient that the first step toward changing thoughts is learning to identify them. It is often difficult at first to become more conscious of the thoughts we are having. However, it is very important to start to try to be aware of those thoughts that are going through our minds that could potentially trigger the cycle of anxiety and panic. You may want to use the following dialogue:

> *For example, while walking into the dance, you might be more aware of the fact that your heart is racing than what thought you are thinking. If this happens, stop for a second and ask yourself, "What is trig-*

gering my heart racing? What am I thinking to myself? Is it possible that this thought is a probability overestimation or that I may be catastrophizing?" Becoming more aware of what you are thinking is a skill and, with practice, you will become very good at being aware of your thoughts.

Review the Thought Record form in Chapter 4 of the workbook. Ask the patient to try to identify triggers of anxiety and panic episodes. Remind him that triggers can be internal (e.g., thoughts, physical sensations) and external (e.g., situations). Instruct the patient to use this form to note his thoughts and beliefs in response to triggers. This should be done for each panic and anxiety episode.

Homework

✎ Have the adolescent review Chapter 4 of the workbook and complete the corresponding quiz.

✎ Instruct the adolescent to record the number of panic attacks and daily levels of anxiety, depression, and pleasantness on the Weekly Record.

✎ Have the adolescent complete a My Cycle of Panic and Anxiety form for each panic attack.

✎ Have the adolescent complete a Thought Record for each panic and anxiety episode experienced over the next week.

Optional Parent Component

Parent(s)/caregiver(s) join the adolescent for the final 10–15 minutes of the session. Use the following agenda:

1. Have the adolescent teach his parents (with therapist assistance as needed) about the following:
   a. cognitive aspects of anxiety (e.g., shark analogy)
   b. cognitive errors (probability overestimation, catastrophic thinking)

2. Discuss and provide Parenting Handout #4: Parenting Anxious Teens, which addresses limit-setting and expecting/anticipating anxiety or anxious situations. Again, stress that parents must present a united front (see Handout #1) and be consistent in their response (see "human slot machine" metaphor in Handout #2), especially in regards to anxious behaviors.

3. Assign homework to the parents along with the adolescent. Parents and adolescent are encouraged to discuss material as they learn it and to complete workbook exercises together.

Chapter 7

Session 4: Cognitive Restructuring (Thinking Like a Detective)

(Corresponds to chapter 5 of the workbook)

Materials Needed

■ Thinking Like a Detective form

Outline

■ Review assigned reading and homework

■ Teach adolescent how to begin thinking like a detective

■ Have adolescent practice countering probability overestimation

■ Have adolescent practice countering catastrophic thinking

■ Discuss myths and misconceptions about anxiety

■ Assign homework

■ Conduct optional parent component

Homework Review

Review the adolescent's study of Chapter 4 of the workbook. Discuss her reaction to this material and the treatment overall. Clarify any immediate questions that arise. Briefly review any homework (e.g., Thought Record). Discuss answers to the quiz and address any questions that the adolescent answered incorrectly.

Thinking Like a Detective

The last session examined common cognitive errors that can contribute to anxiety and panic. This session teaches adolescents how to counter those cognitive errors, which involves "thinking like a detective." Thinking like a detective entails the adolescent truly examining the facts and situations around her (as a detective would), to gain a better understanding of both the realistic probability that something dangerous might occur and her ability to cope if something worrisome did occur. Walk the adolescent through the following steps:

Steps to Thinking Like a Detective:

1. Treat thoughts as hypotheses or guesses, rather than facts.

2. Question/evaluate the evidence that supports and refutes the specific prediction.

3. Explore alternative interpretations of a given situation.

Inform the adolescent that, as she begins to focus on panic-related thoughts (e.g., worry about future panic attacks and the ability to cope with them), she may experience an increase in anxiety because such thoughts are anxiety-provoking. This is normal and to be expected since she may have been avoiding such thoughts for a lengthy period of time. Reassure that adolescent that, as she works through the detective-thinking process, such thoughts will become less salient, less anxiety-provoking, and easier to change.

Also, remind the adolescent that detective-thinking strategies are just like any other skill. They must be practiced before she becomes adept at applying them in panic and anxiety situations.

Countering Probability Overestimation

Choose an example of a specific panic-related probability overestimation made by the adolescent. Use the Thinking Like a Detective form in the workbook to help her to counter the prediction by questioning the evidence (e.g., known facts, past experience or the experience of others, actual probabilities of events) and exploring alternatives. Be sure to give the adolescent examples of questions she can ask herself to counter predictions on her own. These include:

- "How likely is it that my prediction will occur if I panic?"

- "How many times has that happened in the past when I panicked?"

- "What evidence do I have that it will happen? Is there any evidence that it will not happen?"

- "Have I ever seen or heard of that happening to anyone else?"

- "Are there any other possible reasons for these sensations?"

The following example, where T represents the therapist and P represents the patient, illustrates this process of detective thinking for probability overestimation.

T: What anxious thoughts do you have about going to school in the morning?

P: Once I get inside the classroom, I'll have a panic attack and won't be able to breathe.

T: Would not being able to breathe be consistent with what we know about the purpose and activities of the fight-or-flight response?

P: Well, actually, the fight-or-flight response increases breathing, to help prepare the body for action. So, I guess it doesn't make much sense to think that I wouldn't be able to breathe.

T: Is there any evidence that something is wrong with your body that would make you have trouble breathing during a panic attack?

P: I guess not . . .

T: Does your past experience with panic attacks support the thought that you won't be able to breathe?

P: Well, I've probably had hundreds of attacks in my life, but I don't always feel short of breath during an attack. If I only count the attacks when I did feel short of breath, I've probably had about 20. In those, I always felt like I couldn't breathe, but I didn't ever pass out or anything. I did breathe.

T: Then, what do you think the realistic likelihood is that you won't be able to breathe during a panic attack?

P: Well, realistically, it is probably zero. It just feels higher.

T: What is the most likely thing that will happen?

P: Based on previous times, I'll just feel short of breath and probably breathe really, really hard until the attack is over.

Countering Catastrophic Thoughts

Continue teaching the adolescent to think like a detective. A detective-thinking strategy for catastrophic thoughts involves:

1. Imagining the worst consequence actually happening

2. Critical evaluation of the actual severity of the consequence of a "catastrophic" event

The adolescent can ask herself:

- "What is the worst that can happen? How bad is that?"

- "So what if _____ happens?"

- "Could I cope? Have I been able to cope with _____ in the past?"

- "Even if _____ happens, can I live through it?"

- "Is _____ really so terrible?"

The following example, where T represents the therapist and P represents the adolescent patient, illustrates this process of detective thinking for catastrophic thoughts.

T: What is the worst possible thing that could happen if you panicked in this situation?

P: I might faint.

T: Okay. So your first reaction is the prediction that you would faint. What if you did faint? What would happen then?

P: It would be awful.

T: What is it about fainting that would be so terrible?

P: People would think I looked foolish.

T: So, what if people thought you looked foolish? Does it really matter what those people think?

P: Well, no, but I would be so embarrassed.

T: Have you ever been embarrassed before?

P: Yes.

T: Were you able to cope with those feelings of embarrassment and face the same people again?

P: Well . . . yes.

T: What makes you think that you would not be able to cope if you were embarrassed due to panic?

P: It would be very uncomfortable.

T: Well, that may be true, but could you cope with it? Would you be able to live through the embarrassment?

P: I suppose.

T: So, what's so bad about fainting?

P: Nothing really.

It may be useful to inform the adolescent that effective coping does not necessarily imply that the consequence or event will be pleasant or easy. Such events may be uncomfortable and difficult; however, this does not imply that effective coping is impossible.

Discuss with the adolescent that specific catastrophic thoughts are unlikely (e.g., never being able to face people again if embarrassed, never regaining consciousness from fainting), although some events may be likely (e.g., shaking when feeling anxious in a public situation). Stress to the adolescent that anxiety/panic and their effects (e.g., embarrassment) at their worst are *time limited and manageable*.

Therapist Note

▪ *Remember that probability overestimations and catastrophic thoughts are not necessarily mutually exclusive. For example, the adolescent may be overestimating the probability of fainting as a consequence of panic as well as imagining that fainting could be a catastrophe. Such a cognition may be amenable to detective thinking for both types of errors. For example, the adolescent can determine the realistic probability that fainting would actually happen, as well as believing that, if it were to happen, it would not be as bad as she initially thought. Other cognitions may satisfy the criteria for both types of errors, but may be less amenable to one of the detective thinking strategies. For example, thoughts of dying (or going crazy, or having a brain tumor) as a consequence of panic lend themselves very nicely to the detective-thinking strategy used with probability over-estimation. However, such thoughts/events can be very difficult to decatastrophize.* ▪

Using the Thinking Like a Detective form in the workbook, help the adolescent decatastrophize at least one of her catastrophic thoughts related to panic. Whenever possible, refer to information on the causes of anxiety and panic, focusing on the interaction among the three components. Also, you may want to bring the myths and misconceptions covered in the following section into the discussion, if relevant to the adolescent's catastrophic thoughts.

Myths and Misconceptions

Give the adolescent examples of common myths and misconceptions about anxiety (see Chapter 5 of the workbook for a fuller explication). These myths include:

▪ Going Crazy

▪ Losing Control

▪ Nervous Collapse or Fainting

▪ Heart Attack

▪ The Panic Attack Will Never End

Ask the adolescent if she holds any of these myths. Explain that a lack of specific information about and fear of sensations can lead her to form erroneous conclusions about the causes and consequences of the sensations. Discuss the myths and misconceptions relevant to the adolescent, focusing specifically on why they are unlikely to be true.

Homework

✎ Have the adolescent review Chapter 5 of the workbook and complete the corresponding quiz.

✎ Instruct the adolescent to record the number of panic attacks and daily levels of anxiety, depression, and pleasantness on the Weekly Record.

✎ Have the adolescent complete the My Cycle of Panic and Anxiety form for each panic attack.

✎ Have the adolescent counter panic-related probability overestimations and catastrophic thoughts using the Thinking Like a Detective form. It is suggested that the adolescent attempt to add such thoughts to the form once a day, at a regular time and place, to aid in compliance with this homework. However, it may be used more frequently, as needed by the adolescent.

Optional Parent Component

Parent(s)/caregiver(s) join the adolescent for the final 10–15 minutes of the session. Use the following agenda:

1. Have the adolescent teach her parents (with therapist assistance as needed) about the following:
   a. cognitive restructuring (thinking like a detective)
   b. myths and misconceptions

2. Review and discuss the first three parent handouts as needed.

3. Assign homework to the parents along with the adolescent. Parents and adolescent are encouraged to discuss material as they learn it and to complete workbook exercises together.

Chapter 8

Session 5: Interoceptive Exposure (Not Letting How We Feel Scare Us)

(Corresponds to chapter 6 of the workbook)

Materials Needed

- Therapist Interoceptive Exposure Practice Record

- Chair to spin for interoceptive exposure

- Straw to use for interoceptive exposure

- Lamp and paragraph to read for depersonalization exercise

Outline

- Review assigned reading and homework

- Review the physiology of anxiety

- Review the model of panic attacks

- Introduce the concept of interoceptive conditioning

- Explain the rationale for interoceptive exposure

- Conduct symptom induction exercises

- Assign homework

- Conduct optional parent component

Homework Review

Review the adolescent's study of Chapter 5 of the workbook. Discuss his reaction to the treatment. Clarify any immediate questions that arise. Briefly review any homework (e.g., Thinking Like a Detective form). Discuss answers to the quiz and address any questions that the adolescent answered incorrectly.

Review of the Physiology of Anxiety

Briefly review the physiology of anxiety (see Session 2). Remind the adolescent of the following points:

- Anxiety has a survival function; it alerts us to potential danger.

- The sensations experienced during panic reflect the natural physiological processes that are associated with the fight-or-flight response.

- Panic sensations are not harmful in any way. Furthermore, these sensations will eventually dissipate once the fight-or-flight system is no longer activated.

Review of the Model of Panic Attacks

Referring to the Cycle of Panic and Anxiety in Session 1, review the three-component model of anxiety and panic. Panic attacks are a result of the occurrence of certain physical sensations, and fear of the sensations as reflected in one's thoughts and behaviors. These components operate in a vicious cycle in that fear of the sensations increases the intensity of the sensations, which further increases fear, and so on.

Interoceptive Conditioning

Ask the patient if he has ever experienced a panic attack that seemed to come from out of the blue—in other words, when he failed to notice any discernible internal or external trigger for the attack. Explain that one way to explain unexpected panic attacks is the concept of *interoceptive conditioning*. This form of conditioning happens when associations develop between certain sensations and a response of fear or panic. For example, if heart palpitations have been paired with fear many times, then the palpitations can trigger fear without any intervening thoughts or interpretations. The notion of conditioning essentially means that something has become so well learned that the fear response occurs automatically.

Use the following example to illustrate to the adolescent that interoceptive conditioning is learned. Ask the adolescent if he has ever had the experience of becoming sick or vomiting after eating a particular food, and has later felt sick at the mere mention or sight of the food. Taste aversion illustrates the type of conditioning that triggers an automatic reaction, similar to a reaction of fear in response to panic sensations. Other examples include having an automatic reaction to certain smells (e.g., a particular flower) or certain songs/music. Encourage the adolescent to think of other examples of things that elicit an automatic reaction for him.

Implications of Interoceptive Conditioning for Panic Disorder

Discuss how interoceptive conditioning can cause panic to occur in response to very subtle physical sensations. Refer back to the hyperventilation exercise in Session 2 and how even slight changes in breathing can cause sensations of panic. The occurrence of panic for no apparent reason can then result in misinterpretations like the myths presented in Session 4 (e.g., "I must be having a heart attack"; "I'm going crazy").

Certain activities can result in conditioned fear reactions, such as:

- activities that enhance awareness of sensations (e.g., seeing breath in cold air, sweating in hot temperatures)

- activities that produce sensations associated with arousal of the autonomic nervous system (e.g., amusement park rides, physical exercise, excitement)

Ask the patient if he avoids any activities because they elicit sensations associated with panic. Many adolescents with panic disorder limit activities similar to those just noted, but may not have fully realized that this type of avoidance may be due to a reluctance to experience physical sensations that are perceived as aversive or dangerous.

Rationale for Interoceptive Exposure

Explain to the adolescent that since relatively benign and nondangerous internal sensations may be triggering panic reactions, an important component of treatment is to decrease this overreaction to such sensations. By experiencing the feared sensations repeatedly in a controlled way, the patient will begin to separate the experience of physical sensations from the anxiety he feels about the sensations. He will begin to learn that the sensations he has been experiencing during panic attacks are not dangerous or harmful. Therefore, anxiety about such sensations should steadily decrease over time, given the harmless nature of the sensations being experienced.

Emphasize that, for this strategy to be effective at reducing the automatic fear reaction, the adolescent must do the exercises repeatedly until the fear decreases (i.e., he becomes habituated to the sensations). Illustrate this process of habituation (e.g., when learning to ski, a person becomes less fearful with frequent, repeated practice; if he skied only once a year, the fear level would not decrease). Use the metaphor of a wave—the habituation process will bring panic sensations back to baseline levels over time, just like a wave naturally reduces in size as it reaches the shoreline. Like a surfer who might be riding that wave until it naturally brought him back to the shore, emphasize that the adolescent also needs to "ride the wave" of panic until the fear comes down. Use Figure 8.1 to visually illustrate the process of habituation (this figure can also be found in the workbook).

Tell the adolescent that since repeated exposure to the sensations of anxiety and panic is important for habituation to occur, he will be encouraged to eventually stop all attempts at avoiding them. This includes overt attempts to avoid activities and situations that lead to increased

Riding the "wave of anxiety"

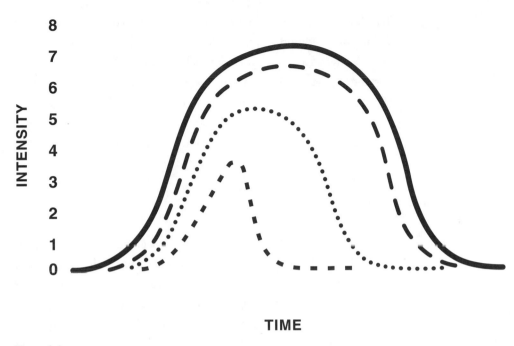

Figure 8.1
Habituation Curve

arousal and/or that elicit sensations (e.g., exercise), and covert attempts (e.g., distraction) to avoid experiencing sensations.

If the adolescent wants to terminate the exposures prematurely:

■ Work toward a compromise; encourage him to try to do as much as he is willing to do.

■ Revisit the rationale for the interoceptive exposures.

■ Increase motivation to participate in the interoceptive exposures by reviewing the reasons why the adolescent is seeking treatment.

■ After the exposure has been completed, attempt to identify the adolescent's thoughts during the exposure and help him determine if these thoughts are accurate.

Management Strategies

Tell the patient that the interoceptive exposures conducted in session will provide additional opportunities to practice using detective thinking (see Session 4) and slow breathing (see Session 2). However, it is important for the adolescent to focus on the sensations first, in order to allow habituation to occur, and not to distract himself away from those sensations, if possible. Instruct the adolescent to only use these strategies after allowing himself to fully experience the sensations.

Symptom Induction Exercises

Inform the patient that the purpose of conducting a variety of symptom-induction exercises is to identify those exercises that elicit sensations most similar to those that naturally occur during his panic attacks. Use the Therapist Interoceptive Exposure Practice Record during the session. A blank copy is provided at the end of this chapter. You may photocopy this form from the book or download multiple copies from the Treatments *ThatWork*™ web site at www.oup.com/us/ttw.

Proceed through each exercise according to the following steps:

1. Briefly demonstrate the exercise.

2. Inform the patient of the duration of the exercise (ranging from 30 seconds to 2 minutes).

3. Have the patient engage in the exercise for the specified duration unless he wants to stop sooner. If this occurs, encourage (but do not force) him to try the exercise again. If the patient refuses to do an exercise despite encouragement, allow him to do so but inform him that an important goal of treatment is for him to be able to engage in the exercise without fear. Thus, at some point, it will be important for him to practice the exercise.

4. After the exercise, obtain the following information and record it on the Therapist Interoceptive Exposure Practice Record:
    ▪ an objective description of the sensations experienced by the adolescent during the exercise

- a rating (0–8) of the intensity of the adolescent's sensations during the exercise
- a rating (0–8) of the intensity of anxiety during the exercise
- a rating (0–8) of the degree of similarity between the sensations experienced during the exercise and those experienced during the adolescent's naturally occurring panic attacks

5. Allow the sensations to at least partially diminish prior to initiating the next exercise.

Specific Exercises

Conduct the following exercises according to the procedure just described. The entire list of exercises should be performed to determine which ones affect the adolescent the most.

Therapist Note

■ *These exercises may cause the patient to experience severe anxiety before the task while worrying about experiencing specified sensations, during the task itself, or after the task if he catastrophizes about the sensations he has just experienced. If this occurs, it is important for the therapist to remain calm and work with the adolescent to both tolerate uncomfortable sensations and, as needed, help correct misinterpretations about the potential consequences of these sensations. If necessary, you may decrease the length and intensity of the exposures; however, you should never give the adolescent excessive reassurance or reinforce the use of other forms of avoidance.* ■

1. Shake head from side to side (does not need to be done quickly) for 30 seconds.

2. Place head between knees for 30 seconds, then quickly lift to an upright position (the patient should experience sensations when the head is lifted).

3. Run in place for 1 minute.

4. Hold breath for 30 seconds.

5. Tense muscles throughout the body for 1 minute or hold a push-up position for as long as possible.

6. Spin in a chair (relatively quickly) for 1 minute.

7. Hyperventilate for 1 minute.

8. Breathe through a thin straw (e.g., a coffee stirrer or cocktail straw) for 2 minutes with nostrils held together.

Individually Tailored Interoceptive Exposure Exercises

If none of the above symptom-induction exercises produced sensations at least moderately similar (i.e., a 4 on the 0–8 point scale) to those that occur during natural panic attacks, individually tailored exercises should be attempted. To create specific sensations, the following exercises are suggested, although some degree of therapist creativity and flexibility may be needed to recreate sensations similar to those most feared by the adolescent.

Chest Pain: Take in a very deep breath and then hyperventilate.

Heat and Sweat: Sit in a very hot room (space heaters may be helpful).

Throat Tightness: Tie a tight scarf, necktie, collar, or the like around the neck.

Choking: Place a tongue depressor on the back part of the tongue or place a finger toward the back of the mouth.

Depersonalization: Stare at a bright light for 1 minute and then read a short paragraph. Alternatively, stare at one's hand for 3 minutes.

If the patient reports little or no fear to any of the exercises, it may be that the adolescent is distracting himself or has the perception of a heightened degree of safety when performing tasks with the therapist or in the therapist's office. If you suspect any of these possibilities, have the adolescent try any or all of the following:

■ Try the exercises while alone in the office.

■ Try the exercise while at home alone. (Be sure the adolescent makes the appropriate ratings.)

■ Try the exercises while imagining experiencing the sensations in an anxiety-provoking situation.

Homework

✎ Have the adolescent review Chapter 6 of the workbook and complete the corresponding quiz.

✎ Instruct the adolescent to record the number of panic attacks and daily levels of anxiety, depression, and pleasantness on the Weekly Record.

✎ Have the adolescent repeat at home on a daily basis the three exercises that induced symptoms closest to his normal sensations of panic. The adolescent should record the results on the Symptom Exposure Record in the workbook.

Optional Parent Component

Parent(s)/caregiver(s) join the adolescent for the final 10–15 minutes of the session. Use the f ollowing agenda:

1. Have the adolescent teach his parents (with therapist assistance as needed) about the following:
   a. interoceptive conditioning
   b. rationale for interoceptive exposure (habituation)

2. Describe the top three interoceptive exposure practices that most closely mimicked what the adolescent experiences when he panics. The adolescent then gets to have each parent experience one of those interoceptive exercises.

3. Discuss and present Parent Handout #4: What To Do (and Not To Do) in the Face of Panic, which addresses the downward spiral of panic and how to react to the adolescent if he is panicking.

4. Assign homework to the parents along with the adolescent. Parents and adolescent are encouraged to discuss material as they learn it and to complete workbook exercises together.

Therapist Interoceptive Exposure Record

Name of Patient: _____

Rating Scale:

0   1   2   3   4   5   6   7   8
None   Moderate   Extreme

Exercise	Sensations	Intensity of Sensation (0–8)	Intensity of Anxiety (0–8)	Similarity to Natural Panic (0–8)
Shake head from side to side for 30 seconds.				
Place head between knees for 30 seconds, then quickly lift to an upright position.				
Run in place for 1 minute.				
Hold breath for 30 seconds.				
Tense muscles throughout the body for 1 minute or hold a push-up position for as long as possible.				
Spin in a chair (relatively quickly) for 1 minute.				
Hyperventilate for 1 minute.				
Breathe through a thin straw for 2 minutes with nostrils held together.				
Other:				

Chapter 9 | *Session 6: Introduction to Situational Exposure*

(Corresponds to chapter 7 of the workbook)

Materials Needed

- Sheet or board to graph habituation exercise
- Fear and Avoidance Hierarchy form
- Therapist Record of Situational Exposure Practice

Outline

- Review assigned reading and homework
- Explain rationale for exposure
- Deal with adolescent's resistance to exposure
- Complete Fear and Avoidance Hierarchy form
- Conduct in-session situational exposure
- Plan for situational exposure
- Assign homework
- Conduct optional parent component

Homework Review

Review the adolescent's study of Chapter 6 of the workbook. Discuss her reaction to the treatment. Clarify any immediate questions that arise. Briefly review any homework (e.g., Symptom Exposure Record).

Discuss answers to the quiz and address any questions that the adolescent answered incorrectly.

Rationale for Exposure

Tell the adolescent that, so far in treatment, we have been focusing mostly on thoughts and sensations. We have discussed how the sensations we experience during anxiety or fear (including panic attacks) can be fully explained by the protective actions of the fight-or-flight response and how these sensations can be exacerbated by hyperventilation. Understanding where these sensations come from and that they are normal and harmless is the first step toward interrupting a potential upward spiral of fear that can result in a panic attack. However, although understanding helps reduce anxious thoughts, it is of limited value in preventing conditioned reactions. In addition, the value of understanding can be completely undone if a person continues to avoid things that cause scary sensations.

Define avoidance broadly as any behavior used to reduce uncomfortable emotions or sensations. This includes overt avoidance (i.e., leaving or not going into anxiety-inducing situations, not engaging in activities that cause panic sensations) as well as more subtle behaviors that make a person feel safer or less anxious in a situation or reduce uncomfortable sensations (e.g., distracting oneself, carrying or taking medication, doing slow breathing). We call these latter behaviors *safety behaviors*. Although they will be discussed further in Session 7, it should be noted that safety behaviors are forms of avoidance, and our aim is to eliminate safety behaviors, especially when doing exposures.

Ask the adolescent what effect avoidance has on a person's fear of a situation. Lead her to conclude (elicit examples if possible) that, although avoidance may provide immediate relief, in the long term it increases anxiety and fear. Guide the adolescent to understand how avoidance increases anxiety and fear in the long term by asking a question such as, "After a long vacation, is it harder or easier to go to school?" Say that most people think it is harder, because they have been away from it for so long. This is similar to how avoidance works—even though it feels good in the short term to avoid the source of anxiety, in the long term, the fear only gets bigger. This is because when a person avoids an anxiety-provoking situation or sensation, she never learns that the situation or sensation is not really dangerous, and never develops confidence in her ability to handle it.

In addition, explain that anxiety and avoidance tend to generalize to other situations and areas of the person's life. For example, if someone avoids going to the movies with friends, for fear of having a panic attack, this avoidance can feel like a relief in the short term. However, the longer someone avoids going to the movies, the harder it is to enter the movie theatre. Often what happens is that adolescents who avoid things like going to the movies soon avoid similar things, like going to a theatre to see a play or concert; this can also start to spread to avoidance of other types of social activities such as going out with others to restaurants or parties. Therefore, what started simply as avoidance of going to the movies can generalize, or spread, to other situations.

Ask the adolescent what the opposite of avoidance is (prompt for facing the feared situation) and if she has had the experience of confronting any panic or general life situations. Lead her to conclude that when a person faces a feared situation repeatedly and for a long enough period, her anxiety comes down. As discussed in Session 5, this decrease in anxiety is called *habituation*. Use the following example to illustrate:

> *For example, think of the last scary movie you saw. Imagine that you watched the movie over and over again, say 50 times. It is very likely that by the 50th time of seeing the scary movie, the things that made you "jump" or feel frightened do not elicit that reaction anymore. This is the concept of habituation.*

Habituation Exercise

Have the adolescent imagine entering one of the most difficult situations that she avoids because of concerns related to panic and doing so not using any avoidance or safety behaviors. Use a dry erase board or piece of paper to draw a graph of the adolescent's anxiety as a function of time leading up to and during the situation. Label anxiety prior to entering the situation as *anticipatory anxiety*. If appropriate, draw one line

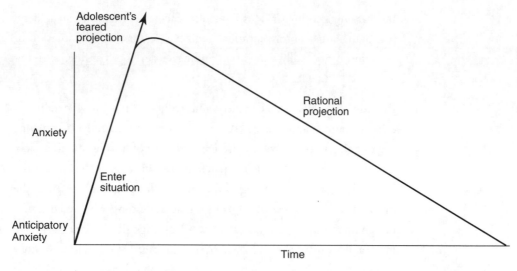

Figure 9.1

Example of Habituation Exercise Graph

to show what the adolescent fears would happen (e.g., anxiety would keep going up or would stay up indefinitely). Draw another line to show what the adolescent rationally thinks would happen. Let the time axis be nonspecific at first. If the adolescent thinks anxiety would come down eventually, ask when. If she thinks it would stay up, ask if it would stay up forever, for a year, a month, or so forth. If necessary, assist the adolescent to challenge probability overestimation using the techniques presented in Session 4. The end-point of this exercise is that the adolescent acknowledges that her anxiety eventually would come down if she remained in the situation, even if she did not use any avoidance or safety behaviors.

Benefits of Facing Fears

After concluding the exercise, explain that when a person repeatedly faces a feared situation, three important things happen from the standpoint of panic disorder (PD):

1.   Her thoughts about the dangerousness of the situation and her ability to cope with it change for the better. This reduces anxiety.

2. Conditioned fear reactions to the situation are weakened and new, healthier associations are created.

3. Avoidance and consequent impairment are eliminated. Because avoidance reinforces fear, this interrupts the panic cycle at the behavioral level.

Stress that because of these positive effects, repeatedly facing fears is a very powerful technique for overcoming agoraphobic fear and avoidance. Moreover, it is the only known way to do it.

Acknowledge that facing avoided situations can be very anxiety provoking and can even trigger panic attacks. However, the experience of those emotions and associated physical sensations is crucial to the effectiveness of exposure therapy because, unless the adolescent learns that she can survive them, she will always fear and avoid them. The stronger the adolescent's anxiety during exposure, the more confidence in her ability to cope she will achieve.

How to Handle Resistance

Emphasize that the next few sessions are the most important ones of treatment, those for which we have been preparing and during which the greatest gains will be made. During the next few weeks, the adolescent will face some of the most difficult situations that can be arranged. It will be hard, but it will be over fairly soon, and you will be there to guide and assist her. The following examples may be helpful:

Just as a surgeon does not scratch at the surface but goes quickly to the site of the problem, so we will progress quickly to some of the more difficult of your situations. We will work together to decide which of these situations to work on and in what order. But, it's important to keep in mind that people literally can change their lives dramatically over a short period of time.

Also like surgery, exposure therapy requires informed consent. Just like a patient can choose to keep a cancerous organ, you can decide to keep living a life restricted by fear. Or, you can choose to courageously endure some amount of pain and discomfort in order to break the back

of panic disorder and recover your health and freedom. We are pro-
viding a unique opportunity, one you are not likely to have again,
but you must decide whether the benefit is worth the cost.

Therapist Note

■ *The specific things/activities that will be done should not be discussed at*
this point. They would only serve to increase anticipatory anxiety and, at
any rate, will depend upon the adolescent's fear and avoidance hierarchy. If
the adolescent asks, say only that you will not ask her to do anything nor-
mal people don't do and that she ultimately can refuse to do anything you
suggest. The adolescent always has the last say. ■

If the adolescent exhibits resistance to doing exposure, you should try
your best to understand and address that, while at the same time being
firm about the absolute necessity of facing fears if the adolescent is to recover. Be careful not to get into a power struggle with the adolescent, because that may cause her to dig in her heels or drop out of treatment. Instead, try to bring her to see the importance of exposure and to commit
to doing it.

Here are some common scenarios of resistance and ways to handle them.

Previous Unsuccessful Attempts at Exposure

If the adolescent says that she has tried exposure before without success,
point out that the approach used in this treatment is markedly different
from attempts the adolescent may have made in the past. Previous attempts may have been unsuccessful for several reasons, including in-
sufficient frequency or duration of exposure practices, the use of avoidance or safety behaviors (including coping strategies), failure to elicit
strong enough sensations, or failure to engage the adolescent's anxious
thoughts. This treatment will address those problems. In addition, the
intensity of the experience and the presence of the therapist during the
initial exposures is much different from past attempts.

Fear of Exposure

If the adolescent expresses fear or doubt about being able to do the exposures, tell her that those concerns are entirely normal among people with PD. Assure her that you will proceed only to the extent she is willing and that she will, in fact, help you to choose the exposure tasks. Also point out that thinking about doing something difficult usually is worse than actually doing it, and that, in your experience, once adolescents taste success, their fear of doing exposures fades. Finally, reiterate that exposure therapy is the only effective way to overcome agoraphobic fear and avoidance. It won't go away on its own.

Excuses for Avoiding Exposures

The adolescent may acknowledge the need to do exposure but give excuses for not going ahead with it now. She may claim that something has come up that prevents her from doing exposures for the time being. Other common excuses are she is under unusual stress at the moment, dealing with withdrawal symptoms of coming off anxiety medication, or not feeling well physically. Note that although other forms of treatment are available, they rarely involve the therapist going with the adolescent into exposure situations. The value of that feature of the current treatment should not be underestimated. Say that, in your experience, the adolescent will be much more likely to succeed if she takes advantage of your assistance. That way you can help her to choose tasks and deal with difficulties that arise. Point out also that if the adolescent thinks she may not be able to succeed under certain adverse circumstances, then that is precisely when she must do it. Otherwise, she will always have doubt and, if similar circumstances arise in the future, she will be at risk for lapsing.

General Hesitation about Exposure

The adolescent may acknowledge the preceding arguments, but still be unsure about whether to proceed. Tell her to think carefully about it before the next session, read the next chapter of the workbook, and talk with family members or friends before deciding. She can let you know at the next session.

If the adolescent says she does not want to go ahead with exposure, tell her that the choice is entirely up to her. Don't try to badger her into doing something she doesn't want to do. Rather, present the situation to the adolescent diplomatically:

> So, then, here is where we are. You acknowledge that your agoraphobia is restricting your life, and you understand that the only way to overcome it is to confront your fears head-on. You understand, too, that treatments generally do not provide for the therapist to accompany you on exposures, so that this is a rare opportunity. Nevertheless, at this point in time, you prefer not to continue in this treatment. Naturally, the choice is entirely up to you, and I will respect your decision. Still, take the coming week to think it over again, and if you feel the same way by the next session, we can talk about alternative choices for therapy or support.

Fear and Avoidance Hierarchy

Together with the adolescent, complete the Fear and Avoidance Hierarchy (FAH) form in the workbook by rank ordering 10 situations that she tends to avoid due to fear of having a panic attack. Also have the adolescent complete avoidance and fear ratings for each situation on the FAH. Keep a copy of the adolescent's FAH for reference.

The situations should be those that the adolescent could reasonably practice during the course of treatment. Some exposures will be completed by the adolescent with a therapist, others by the adolescent alone, and still others will be completed by the adolescent with her parents.

The adolescent should choose some activities that are more difficult and some practices that are easier. The aim is to help the adolescent feel that she could start somewhere on the list and be successful at an attempt to enter one of the situations. It is important that the adolescent think of ways to make each situation harder, even if those variants might not be regularly encountered. For example, if going to the movies is on the list, add "while sitting in the middle of the middle row, during a crowded time, in the evening." Each of those qualifiers is meant to add difficulty to the situation. Keep in mind that what is difficult for one adolescent will be different from what is difficult for another.

In-Session Situational Exposure

See Chapter 11 for full instructions on how to conduct situational exposures. Instruct the patient on the procedure to be used. Use the Therapist Record of Situational Exposure Practice provided at the end of this chapter to keep track of the exposures completed in session. You may photocopy this form from the book or download multiple copies from the Treatments *ThatWork*™ web site at www.oup.com/us/ttw.

Choose a situation from the adolescent's FAH to practice in session. It is desirable for the patient to experience success initially. Choose the hardest thing that you think the patient can accomplish with your accompaniment. Invariably, this should be something the patient thinks she *cannot* do. The more difficult the task, the greater the patient's sense of accomplishment and optimism will be afterward. Also, starting high on the hierarchy will save time. Since you will be along at first, you can generally choose something near the top of the patient's hierarchy.

Try to start with something near the office, so there is less time for anticipatory anxiety to build. For the same reason, try not to give away what you will be doing until you get there. Also, it is best to start with something that is more difficult to escape (e.g., taking an elevator as opposed to driving) as a first exposure.

Therapist Note

▪ *Realize that your patient is an adolescent who may have personal issues or immediate concerns that she would like to address (e.g., going to the prom, oral report for school, etc.). Take time to listen to the adolescent and incorporate these issues into treatment when possible. For example, if the adolescent is anxious about attending her prom, discuss what exposures she can do to prepare. It is important to keep sessions focused and on-task; however, it is also extremely important that you are sensitive to adolescent issues. If possible, address adolescent concerns while weaving in skills/themes from treatment. For example, if nervous about a prom, you could walk the adolescent through restructuring anxious thoughts about her prom.* ■

Planning for Situational Exposure

Encourage the adolescent to start exposures on her own before the next session if she feels able to. Help the adolescent pick appropriate exposures from the FAH as homework; remember that situational exposure should begin with the less anxiety-provoking situations on the hierarchy and progress to the most anxiety-provoking situations during the course of treatment.

Assist the adolescent in making any necessary plans or preparations for the homework exposures. Instruct the adolescent to apply the information and skills learned thus far in treatment to the situational exposure, and to record anxiety, thoughts, and behaviors on the Situational Exposure Record in the workbook. She can record any other feelings or notes in the comments section of the form.

Also, remind the adolescent to bring to the next session whatever money, clothing, and the like that you think may be needed for exposures.

Homework

✎ Have the adolescent review Chapter 7 of the workbook and complete the corresponding quiz.

✎ Instruct the adolescent to record the number of panic attacks and daily levels of anxiety, depression, and pleasantness on the Weekly Record.

✎ Have the adolescent complete a My Cycle of Panic and Anxiety form for each panic attack.

✎ Have the adolescent repeat in-session exposure at home and record it on the Situational Exposure Record.

✎ Have the adolescent enter situations from the FAH as planned and record them on the Situational Exposure Record.

Optional Parent Component

Parent(s)/caregiver(s) join the adolescent for the beginning as well as the end of the session. Use the following agenda:

1. At the beginning of the session, if possible, have parents available for a low-level exposure—preferably something in or around the building. They should see you model setting up the exposure and handling the adolescent's anxiety. Emphasize that it is important that they understand what you're doing, as they will be taking over coaching their child through exposures after therapy has ended.

2. At the end of the session, have the parents join the session for approximately 15–20 minutes. Have the adolescent tell her parents about all of the exposures that occurred during the day. If the adolescent does not do so herself, be sure to brag about all of the impressive feats she accomplished.

3. Inform parents that the adolescent had a stressful day and may be tired, irritable, or anxious. Although they do not need to handle the adolescent with kid gloves, they should be empathic to the trying day she has had and should not be surprised if she has more panic symptoms than the day prior—this is actually a good sign because it means the adolescent is facing her fears and no longer avoiding them!

4. Ask about any panic attacks or symptoms the adolescent experienced with the parents during the last week and how they responded. Remind them about the suggestions in Parent Handout #4: What To Do (and Not To Do) in the Face of Panic.

5. Assign homework to the parents along with the adolescent. Parents and adolescent are encouraged to discuss material as they learn it and to complete workbook exercises together.

6. Make plans for the week regarding what exposures the adolescent is going to conduct with her parents.

Therapist Record of Situational Exposure Practice

Name of Patient: _____

Rating Scale:

0   1   2   3   4   5   6   7   8
None   Moderate   Extreme

Date	Situation	Trial #	Intensity of Physical Sensation (0–8)	Maximum Anxiety (0–8)

Chapter 10   *Session 7: Safety Behaviors and Exposures*

(Corresponds to chapter 7 of the workbook)

Materials Needed

■ Copy of adolescent's Fear and Avoidance Hierarchy (FAH) form

■ Therapist Record of Situational Exposure Practice

Outline

■ Review assigned reading and homework

■ Review safety behaviors

■ Discuss rationale for eliminating safety behaviors

■ List adolescent's safety behaviors

■ Plan for situational exposure

■ Conduct situational exposure

■ Assign homework

■ Conduct optional parent component

Homework Review

Review the adolescent's study of Chapter 7 of the workbook. Discuss adolescent's reaction to the treatment. Clarify any immediate questions that arise. Briefly review any homework (e.g., Situational Exposure Record). Discuss answers to the quiz and address any questions that the adolescent answered incorrectly.

Safety Behaviors

As discussed in the last session, safety behaviors are things a person does to make him feel safer or less anxious in a situation or to reduce uncomfortable sensations. Review common safety behaviors with the adolescent. These include:

- distracting oneself

- carrying or taking medication

- doing relaxation or slow breathing

- having to be with someone

- bringing along a water bottle, cell phone, etc.

Rationale for Eliminating Safety Behaviors

Although safety behaviors may make it possible for a person to enter or stay in a situation rather than avoid or escape it altogether, they do keep him from completely facing the situation. Also, the use of safety behaviors only perpetuates the anxiety and makes it worse in the long run, because patients are not allowing themselves to fully experience the symptoms of anxiety.

Note that safety behaviors—including breathing, relaxation, cognitive countering, and other behaviors the adolescent uses—may be considered adaptive coping strategies under normal conditions; however, since their purpose is to reduce anxiety or uncomfortable sensations they are not to be used during exposures.

Therapist Note

- *This last point may be surprising and confusing to the patient. To explain, point out that coping behaviors that act to reduce fear or scary sensations in a situation may be helpful in the short run but, like helpful medications, they also have some undesirable effects.*

By protecting the adolescent from experiencing the full extent of the fear or sensations elicited by the situation, these coping behaviors prevent him from gathering evidence that is crucial to disproving his cata-strophic predictions about what might happen in the situation if his panic went unchecked. Consequently, the patient is unable to develop confidence that the fear or sensations elicited by the situation—and hence the situation itself—are not dangerous. In that regard, these cop-ing behaviors are similar to other avoidance or safety behaviors. Even if the patient remains in the situation, there will always be doubt at some level as to whether the anxiety or sensations would have been dangerous if the patient had not kept them under control. That seed of doubt will act to maintain the adolescent's fear.

To keep that from happening, it will be necessary for the patient *not* to use those behaviors (or any other avoidance or safety behaviors) *during exposure tasks.*

Listing Safety Behaviors

Now that the adolescent has a full understanding of safety behaviors, help him list his own safety behaviors, including coping strategies, in the space provided in the workbook. If the patient still objects to listing these strategies with more maladaptive behaviors, he can mark them with an asterisk to indicate their dual nature. Review the list with the pa-tient and discuss how he can keep from using those behaviors during ex-posure practice.

Planning for Situational Exposures

Prior to this session, you should give some thought to the exposures you will do with the patient. From your review of the patient's pretreatment Anxiety Disorders Interview Schedule (ADIS) and the preceding cogni-tive-behavioral therapy sessions, you should by now have a good idea of tasks that would be appropriate. Some of those may require advance planning (e.g., checking schedules, deciding on the need for a car, get-ting directions or a map). If so, that should be done before you start today, so as not to lose time in session. Your plans will be refined—and possibly changed—when you meet with the patient and go over his fear and avoidance hierarchy, so allow for flexibility. Tasks that need firm schedules (e.g., appointments or reservations) are best done during the next exposure session, after you have seen how well the patient does in this session.

The first part of the session is done in the office (review, rationale, and listing of safety behaviors). After that, you and the patient will go to wherever the exposures are to be done.

Therapist Note

■ *Do not discuss the plan with the patient. If he asks, tell him you will be improvising as you go along, in collaboration with him.* ■

In formulating the plan, several aspects of the tasks should be considered:

Ease of Putting Tasks Together

Once you start exposures, you will want to take advantage of successes to build momentum. As soon as the patient accomplishes one task, you should move quickly to the next, or do two or more in parallel. For example, if the patient gets on the subway and goes one stop without you, the next exposure might be going five stops without you, and then doing an exposure that involves the patient switching trains and then meeting you at an agreed-upon location.

Difficulty of the Task

It is necessary for the patient to feel anxious for exposure to work (so that habituation can be experienced), but he should not be so anxious or panicky that he refuses to do the task or stops it prematurely. The general guideline is to make the task as challenging as possible yet still doable—something that the patient will find difficult and that he generally avoids or does only with safety behaviors. It does not have to be a situation at the very top of the hierarchy. It is often helpful for adolescents to build up some confidence and trust with their therapist about the way exposures will be practiced. However, the goal is to experience symptoms and to let habituation occur. The patient should understand this general goal. To achieve it requires fine-tuning in specifying the task.

Use of Avoidance and Safety Behaviors

For the reasons noted earlier, exposure ultimately must be done without any behaviors (including slow breathing) that reduce the patient's full experience of the anxiety or scary sensations elicited by the task. It is best if the task can be done without such behaviors from the start. If that proves to be impossible, fade the safety behaviors out as quickly as possible. For example, this can be done by taking away the patient's water bottle, cell phone, or anything else listed on his safety behaviors sheet. This also includes fading out your own presence.

Duration of the Task

The objective of exposure tasks is to confront the feared situation long enough and/or often enough that it ceases to be scary. Individual practices must be continued until the patient's anxiety peaks and then comes down. If the patient terminates a task before his anxiety has come down, the practice will potentially be counterproductive. In that case, the patient is likely to conclude that his anxiety stays up (or worse, continues to increase) as long as he remains in the situation and is relieved only by escape. The patient must understand this point clearly: *practices will be helpful only if they are continued to the point that anxiety decreases*. Because the amount of time that takes will vary, the duration of practices must be based on achieving that outcome, rather than on a predetermined time period.

In most instances, 90 minutes is sufficient for habituation to occur. Some tasks will take much less time. Occasionally, some may take longer, particularly if the patient keeps scaring himself with catastrophic thoughts during the practice. Tasks that are too brief for anxiety to come down in a single execution (e.g., driving across a bridge or between two exits on a limited-access highway) should be done repeatedly in each practice session until anxiety decreases (e.g., driving back and forth across a bridge or over the same stretch of road).

Incorporation of Symptom-Induction Procedures

Unlike specific phobias, in which the phobic stimulus itself is the focus of the fear reaction, in agoraphobia, it is the occurrence of scary *sensations* in a situation that is the usual trigger for fear or avoidance of the situation. For the agoraphobic patient to be able to overcome his fear of the situation, he must be able to remain in it while experiencing those sensations and see that the predicted catastrophe does not occur. That is the necessary condition for exposure therapy to work for agoraphobia. The more intense the sensations that are endured, the greater the sense of mastery the patient will achieve.

When doing situational exposure tasks, it is important for the patient to experience sensations like those that occur during panic attacks. This may happen naturally if the task is difficult enough. However, once the patient has habituated to a task, scary symptoms should be augmented by adding symptom-induction procedures to the task. Deliberately increasing scary sensations is the opposite of using avoidance and safety behaviors and has the reverse effect—namely, it shows the patient that there is nothing to fear, even if sensations are intense.

The patient may have difficulty understanding this concept. Typically, patients think that the goal is to complete exposure tasks with as little anxiety as possible. While it is true that the ultimate goal of treatment is for the patient to be able to resume avoided activities without undue anxiety, the patient must realize that the *only way to accomplish that is to overcome fear of having a panic attack* during an activity. That means being willing to face the worst-case scenario. This concept should be discussed with the patient, and he should be instructed to deliberately intensify sensations during situational exposure tasks.

In-session Exposure

See Chapter 11 for the full instructions on how to conduct exposures. Use the Therapist Record of Situational Exposure Practice provided at the end of Chapter 9 to keep track of the exposures completed in session. You may photocopy this form from the book or download multiple copies from the Treatments *ThatWork*™ web site at www.oup.com/us/ttw.

Homework

✎ The adolescent should have already read Chapter 7 of the workbook and completed the corresponding quiz. Have him review exposure guidelines as needed.

✎ Instruct the adolescent to record the number of panic attacks and daily levels of anxiety, depression, and pleasantness on the Weekly Record.

✎ Have the adolescent complete a My Cycle of Panic and Anxiety form for each panic attack.

✎ Have the adolescent review his list of safety behaviors.

✎ Have the adolescent repeat in-session exposure at home and record it on the Situational Exposure Record.

✎ Have the adolescent enter situations from the FAH as planned and record them on the Situational Exposure Record.

Optional Parent Component

As in Session 6, parent(s)/caregiver(s) join the adolescent for the beginning as well as the end of the session. Use the following agenda:

1. At the beginning of the session, if possible, have parents available for a low- to medium-level exposure—preferably something in or around the building. They should again watch you model setting up the exposure and handling the adolescent's anxiety. Re-emphasize that as the future coaches of their child, it is important that they understand what you're doing.

2. At the end of the session, have the parents join the session for approximately 15–20 minutes. Have the adolescent tell his parents about all of the exposures that occurred during the day. If the adolescent does not do so himself, be sure to brag about all of the impressive feats he accomplished.

3. Remind parents that the adolescent had a stressful day and may be tired, irritable, or anxious. Although they do not need to handle the adolescent with kid gloves, they should be empathic to

the trying day he has had and should not be surprised if his panic symptoms are worse than they were the day prior.

4. Ask about any panic attacks or symptoms the adolescent experienced with the parents in the last week and how they responded. Remind them about the suggestions in Parent Handout #4: What To Do (and Not To Do) in the Face of Panic.

5. Make plans for the week regarding what exposures the adolescent is going to conduct with his parents. Particularly for older teens, or those for whom the parents are safety objects, design some reasonable exposures for the teen to conduct alone. Help the family create a reasonable, but challenging, schedule for exposures and emphasize rewarding the adolescent's accomplishments.

Chapter 11 | *Sessions 8–10: Exposure Sessions*

(Corresponds to chapter 7 of the workbook)

Materials Needed

- Copy of adolescent's Fear and Avoidance Hierarchy (FAH) form

- Therapist Record of Situational Exposure Practice

Outline

- Review homework exposures

- Review the patient's FAH form

- Review the exposure procedure

- Conduct exposures

- Review adolescent's progress after exposures

- Troubleshoot for extreme emotions and delaying tactics

- Plan for homework exposures

- Assign homework

- Conduct optional parent component

Homework Review

Review the exposures completed by the patient, and congratulate her on her accomplishments. If the patient had problems, review them and how she handled them, and provide corrective feedback as appropriate.

Assist the patient to use her experiences (both successes and failures) as evidence to challenge anxious thoughts and catastrophic predictions.

Over the course of the next three sessions, you will work with the patient to conduct more exposures, working up to the most difficult situations on her FAH form.

Fear and Avoidance Hierarchy Review

Every effort should be made to get the patient to the top of her FAH by the end of Session 10, if this is practical. Some things (e.g., overnight travel) are hard to do in session yet, with some planning, these exposures can be assigned as homework or can be conducted as part of in-session exposures.

After Session 7, you should have a better idea of what the patient will be able to do. Therefore, you can do things that will require advance scheduling (e.g., going horseback riding, taking a ferry trip or flight) for Sessions 8–10. You may want to make necessary arrangements or reservations in advance.

As the sessions continue, you should let the patient do more on her own, while encouraging her to move toward practicing the highest practical item on her hierarchy. That is the overriding goal. Keep in mind that you will be asking the patient to do unaccompanied exposures as homework; work toward that by fading out your accompaniment during the session.

Therapist Note

■ *The exposure sessions require a fair amount of flexibility on the part of the therapist. If you face time restrictions at your clinic, be sure to plan exposures so they can be successfully completed (i.e., the patient habituates) in the time allotted. If you are short on time, make the most of exposures by using symptom induction.* ■

Exposure Procedure

Prior to the first exposure, instruct the patient on the procedure to be used. Right before the exposure, the adolescent may drink caffeine or engage in a interoceptive exercise aimed at increasing physical sensations. Next, the patient chooses an exposure exercise and makes sure not to utilize avoidance techniques or safety behaviors during the exposure. It is important for the adolescent to stay in the situation until her anxiety habituates or comes down. The patient can then try to vary the exercise slightly to make it harder (e.g., do an interoceptive exercise prior to going to a movie). When the adolescent succeeds at an exposure, it is important for her to use self-praise and to feel good about her accomplishments.

Therapist Accompaniment

Tell the patient that you will be accompanying her on tasks initially, to observe and coach her until she develops sufficient confidence to do a task alone. Generally, your withdrawal will be gradual; that is, you will remove yourself a little at a time.

Riding the Wave of Anxiety

Ask the patient to let the anxiety wash over her without resistance during exposures. Remind her that this is not harmful. She should allow herself to feel the sensations that occur as a result of activation of the autonomic nervous system, notice the thoughts they evoke, and observe how she is behaving. Say that it is almost like riding a wave: feel the anxiety rise and then dissipate.

Therapist Interaction

Inform the patient that you will be asking her to rate her anxiety periodically during exposures, so that you can monitor changes over time (you may want to develop a system for doing this unobtrusively in public situations). For example, you can say the word "number" or some other agreed-upon word or phrase, and the patient can either write the number of her anxiety rating on a piece of paper or say it aloud. You may also make occasional suggestions or comments relevant to the task.

Otherwise, you will not talk to her during exposures, because that would serve as a distraction or safety signal.

Making Tasks More Difficult

Stress to the patient that the exposures will be effective to the extent that the patient experiences anxiety/panic and related sensations to the fullest. You will be relying on the patient to suggest ways to make tasks harder. Explain that patients are naturally reluctant to do that, and it is perfectly possible for them to do subtle things to reduce their fear or feel safer. But if they do, they will only hurt themselves in the long run.

Panic Attacks

If, during the course of an exposure, the patient experiences a panic attack, instruct her to stay in the situation and ride it out. Panic attacks enable the patient to test her catastrophic predictions and gain confidence in her ability to survive even the worst-case scenario. Ultimately, the patient must acquire that confidence, or she will continue to be afraid.

Anger

Warn the patient that when people feel cornered, the fight-or-flight system switches from the escape mode (flight) to defense (fight). When that happens, people often notice it as anger. It is likely that the patient will feel anger with you at times during the next couple weeks. That is good, because it means that she is pushing herself to the limit of her fear, which is where the most progress will be made.

Maximizing the Chances That Anxiety Will Be Experienced

You will need to take measures to ensure that the patient experiences anxiety during exposures. Ask the patient to surrender any safety objects she has with her. You will leave them in the office today. In addition, if the patient avoids caffeine because it makes her anxious, request that she drink some caffeinated water before you start out. Check that the patient understands the rationale for these and is willing to do them.

Be prepared to use other means as well, if pertinent to anxiety, to increase scary sensations (e.g., have the patient put on uncomfortably warm clothing or a tight scarf, eat a lot of spicy food). **Note:** *PRN anxiolytic medications should not be allowed.*

Conducting Exposures

Use the Therapist Record of Situational Exposure Practice provided at the end of Chapter 9 to keep track of the exposures completed during each session. You may photocopy this form from the book or download multiple copies from the Treatments *ThatWork*™ web site at www.oup.com/us/ttw. Your goal for these sessions is to assist the patient in doing as many exposures from her hierarchy as possible, consistent with the procedure previously outlined. In addition, the following general guidelines should govern your conduct during exposures.

Be supportive and warm, but firm. You should convey a sense of confidence that the patient will succeed, while acknowledging the difficulty of the task and the patient's courage in undertaking it.

Before each exposure, ask the patient to predict what will happen. Afterwards, ask about the nature and intensity of the sensations the patient experienced, any anxious thoughts she had, and any avoidance or safety behaviors or other coping strategies she used. Assist the patient in using the experience to revise her predictions and plan the next exposure task. For example, if the patient used an avoidance or safety behavior, ask what she thinks would happen if she did the opposite next time, and then have her repeat the exposure. That is:

■ If the patient did anything to make herself feel less anxious or safer, or to reduce scary sensations, then she should do the exposure again without that behavior.

■ If the patient can think of anything that would make her feel more anxious or less safe, or would increase scary sensations, then she should do the exposure again with those thoughts in mind.

During exposures, keep conversation to a minimum. Approximately every 5 minutes, ask the patient for a rating (0–8) of her anxiety or fear. You should also point out any avoidance or safety behaviors that you observe the patient use. Example: "I notice that you are touching the wall. Does that make you feel safer? If so, can you step away from the wall?" Be on the alert for subtle behaviors.

If the patient says she can't stay in a situation any longer, you may give gentle encouragement. Example: "It is only your fear. Stay with it. It will not hurt you. You can do this." If that is not enough, it is better to allow the patient to use an avoidance or safety behavior (e.g., receiving your assistance) to stay in a situation than to leave the situation before habituation has begun. Example: "Wait. Hang on to me, and tell me what you are afraid will happen. I am here with you. We are perfectly safe. We can fight this together." If the patient can recover with your help, review the outcome and then encourage her to do the task again without your help.

If the patient stops a task prematurely due to excessive anxiety, be supportive. Congratulate her on staying with it as long as she did, and then process what happened that made her leave. Critically review what happened, aside from the anxiety. Even though the patient aborted the task, it is unlikely that the events she most feared would happen actually did occur. Assist her to review again the evidence for and against her fears and try to arrive at rational alternative thoughts. Give her a little time to regain composure and then encourage her to try the task again. If she is too afraid to do the same task again, change it to make it a little easier or pick an easier task, something she should be able to do. Try to give her a success to offset the failure. Return to the failed task later, when she is willing.

As a general rule, do not end an exposure until the patient has experienced some degree of habituation, as indicated by a decrease of anxiety.

After each exposure:

■ Praise the patient for her accomplishment

■ Review the patient's anxiety ratings (it may be helpful to graph these)

- If the patient habituated, use that as evidence that facing anxiety results in a decrease in anxiety

- If the patient did not habituate, examine the reasons (e.g., exposure not long enough, subtle avoidance behaviors, repeatedly scaring self)

Follow up successes with new challenges. Example: "That's great. You did it! Now what could you do to make it harder?" Or: "That was terrific. Now do it again, but this time hyperventilate and spin in place while you do it." Always challenge the patient to do more than she thinks she can do (e.g., have her go four extra floors on the elevator, ride three extra subway stops, drive two more exits on the highway, etc.).

Fade out your presence as soon as you think it is possible. This should be done sooner than the patient thinks is reasonable. Do this in steps. For example, for driving exposures, you can first ride in the back seat (with the mirror adjusted so that the patient can't see you), then get out and have the patient drive around the block without you, then have the patient leave you somewhere (e.g., near a subway or bus stop) and meet you at a designated place and time (e.g., back at the office, or at a place where you will be doing the next exposure). For extra difficulty, the designated place can be somewhere unfamiliar to the patient, so that she will need to get directions or follow a map.

After Exposures

Review of Accomplishments

At the end of exposures, meet with the patient to review her accomplishments. Do this in detail, so that the patient can appreciate her progress. For example:

> So you mean to tell me that you drank four cups of coffee through the day, rode the subway alone to the mall, ran from the subway to the mall, ate spicy food, and spent 2 hours alone shopping in the mall? Could you have imagined yesterday that you could have done that?

Sometimes, patients are reluctant to take credit, because they were anxious the whole time or had a panic attack or didn't enjoy it. They might express discouragement that it is so hard for them to do things everyone else finds easy. If that happens, reframe the cognitions by pointing out that anxiety is the goal of exposures, the more the better. If it hadn't been hard or they hadn't felt panicky, the exposures would have been useless. There will be time enough later to enjoy things, but during treatment, the patient should strive to feel and face as much anxiety as possible.

Normalizing Exhaustion and Apprehension

Typically, patients (and therapists) feel emotionally and physically exhausted by the end of the session. They may complain of headaches, soreness, lack of appetite, or other physical symptoms consistent with a very stressful day. Normalize this for the patient; you may want to use the following dialogue:

> *After what you have been through today, it would be a miracle if you didn't feel that way. Imagine how a football player feels at the end of a grueling game. In a way, your feelings are a sign that you gave it your all; you can be proud of them. Now go home, do something nice to reward yourself, and get some rest.*

If the patient expresses apprehension about doing more exposures, normalize that as well. To reassure the patient, the following script might be useful:

> *Patients often feel a period of let-down at this point. Your adrenaline has been working overtime all day, and now that the demand is over, it is normal to crash. Under those conditions, it's natural to think you don't have the energy to do it again. Don't let your exhaustion mislead you. In our experience, patients find they do have the energy and are, in fact, surprised that things that were so hard today are easier the next time around.*

Extreme Emotions

When faced with something they are terrified to do, it is not uncommon for patients to cry, yell, plead, say they have accomplished enough, threaten to quit, or in short, say anything that might get them a reprieve. At the same time, you may have emotions of your own. It is difficult to know that you are the cause of the patient's distress and natural to want to ease it. You may feel conflicted. You may question whether it really is necessary to push so hard or worry that a bad experience now could undo the progress the patient has made. You may not want the patient to see you as cruel, uncaring, or even sadistic. You may rationalize that the patient now knows how to do exposures, that it works, and she can finish the remaining tasks on her own.

Usually, there comes a point during exposure, perhaps more than one, when you are strongly tempted to back off. These can be turning points in the treatment, times that you and your patient will look back on as critical. You should anticipate them and be prepared to handle them. Here are some suggestions:

Acknowledge the Difficulty of Exposure

First, it is important to acknowledge the difficulty of what you are asking the patient to do. Often patients tell us afterward that this treatment was the hardest thing they have ever done. Let the patient know that you appreciate how hard it is and don't think she is simply weak, difficult, resistant, or something else negative.

Recognize the Necessity of Exposure

Keep in mind that, as much as the patient wishes there were an easier way, on another level, she recognizes that going ahead is the only way to overcome her fear. She knew that when she undertook the treatment, and she still does. The same pertains to you. As much as you may wish there were an easier way, you know there isn't. You should discuss this frankly with the patient.

Stand Firm

Stand firm in the importance of pressing ahead. Patients have told us that, if they had thought the therapist might relent, they would have taken advantage of that to get out of a difficult task. Any signs of ambivalence or uncertainty on your part will only prolong the crisis and add to the patient's fear. You must convey absolute confidence that this is the right thing to do and express your belief that the patient can handle it.

Control the Discussion

Don't let the discussion go on too long. If you do, the patient will use it as a tactic to avoid doing the exposure. Moreover, she will be engaging in confidence-destroying arguments that will make her even more afraid. Don't let that happen. Instead, just run through the points in the preceding paragraphs and then tell the patient the decision is hers. For example:

> *I know that what I am asking you to do is terrifying. I wish there were an easier way. But we both know there isn't. Facing your fears fully, being willing to risk the worst, is the only way to overcome them. Avoidance is what you have been doing until now, and it hasn't worked. You began this treatment because you wanted to change that, and we have been working toward this moment since the beginning. I know that you can do this, even though it terrifies you, and that if you do, it will make you stronger. If you quit now, you will lose a rare opportunity. But it is your life, and the choice is yours. We can quit now and go home or take the next step. You tell me which it will be.*

Don't badger the patient, but on the other hand, don't make it easy for her to quit. Prolonging the discussion beyond the preceding dialogue probably is unwise. Instead, having said something like that, leave the patient to think it over. Example: "I am going to sit in the car (or on that bench, etc.) while you decide what you want to do. Let me know when you have decided."

Negotiate

At this point, the patient may try for a compromise. Don't offer one yourself, and try to hold out for the original task, but if the patient flatly refuses to do it, then be willing to negotiate. Don't accept the patient's first offer; try to up the ante.

Prepare for Anger

Be prepared for anger, and don't take it personally. It is the "fight" side of the fight-or-flight reaction. Point out to the patient that it is an indication that she feels cornered. Then remind her that she isn't cornered. This is a collaborative treatment, and the patient has a say in what happens. It is true that you will be challenging her to go farther than she wants to, but you can't make her do that. Ultimately, she has the control.

Delaying Tactics

Keep in mind that the goals for today are exposure and habituation. Even though they accept the need for exposure, patients understandably tend to want to put off the discomfort. Or, they may worry you are going too fast or that they aren't quite ready yet. Consequently, they may try delaying tactics.

Conversation is a common one. In addition to delaying exposures, it serves as a distraction from anxiety. Keep talk to a minimum during exposures. If the patient wants to socialize, say you would like that too, but possibly on the way home, after the exposures are finished. For now, you want her to concentrate on the exposures.

Sometimes, patients will use cognitive restructuring as a delaying tactic. It is good before an exposure to ask what the patient thinks will happen (i.e., her predictions) and to check these afterward, but keep this brief. Use cognitive restructuring only as necessary to get the patient to do the exposure. Instead of restructuring a catastrophic prediction, challenge the patient to test it by doing the exposure.

Occasionally, a patient will complain of feeling unwell, or of a preexisting medical problem worsening, necessitating a break or a slower pace. Evaluate these complaints critically and ask the patient to honestly consider whether she might be welcoming the symptoms as an acceptable reason for avoidance. If the patient has a medical condition that could affect the types of exposures you do, that should have been identified prior to treatment and the exposures designed accordingly (see Chapter 13 for suggested modifications for asthma). If there is any question about this, consult with the patient's physician before planning the day. On the other hand, a patient who simply feels tired or unwell is not a reason to slow down. On the contrary, point out that those are the best times to do an exposure, because the objective is for the patient to learn that she can manage even under the worst conditions.

Planning for Homework Exposures

At the end of each session, meet with the patient to review progress, congratulate her on accomplishments, and plan for homework exposures.

Emphasize the pivotal nature of the exposure phase of treatment. Stress to the patient that homework exposures are as important or more so than anything she has done thus far. They mark the transition from dependence on the therapist to true independence. Just because you are not along, the patient should not be any less aggressive or demanding in doing exposures than she has been during sessions. Exposures should be done in the same way, and for the entire day.

Review of Exposure Principles

When assigning homework exposures, review the principles detailed in Session 4. They may be summarized in the following general rule:

Exposures will be more beneficial to the extent that they are

- more difficult,

- done without any avoidance or safety behaviors,

- continued until anxiety and fear subside,

- done more often, and

- accompanied by more intense panic-like sensations.

Ensure that the patient understands and accepts these aims, and encourage her to strive to achieve them during exposure practices.

Review of Exposure Procedure

For homework exposures, the patient should follow the same procedure listed in this chapter, except that she will be conducting exposures on her own. Direct the patient's attention to the version of the exposure guidelines outlined in Chapter 7 of the workbook.

Homework

- ✎ The adolescent should have already read Chapter 7 of the workbook and completed the corresponding quiz. Have her review exposure instructions as needed during the remaining exposure sessions.

- ✎ Instruct the adolescent to record the number of panic attacks and daily levels of anxiety, depression, and pleasantness on the Weekly Record.

- ✎ Have the adolescent complete a My Cycle of Panic and Anxiety form for each panic attack.

- ✎ Have the adolescent enter situations from the FAH as planned and record them on the Situational Exposure Record.

Parent(s)/caregiver(s) join the adolescent for the beginning as well as the end of Sessions 8–10. Use the following agenda:

1. Start each session with parents and the adolescent in the room to debrief about last week's homework exposures. Once they've shared stories and problem-solved any difficulties that may have arisen, parents can leave until the end of the session.

2. At the end of each session, have the parents join the session for approximately 15–20 minutes. Have the teen tell her parents about all of the exposures that occurred during the day. If she does not do so herself, be sure to brag about all of the impressive feats she accomplished.

3. Remind parents that their child had a stressful day and may be tired, irritable, or anxious. Although they do not need to handle her with kid gloves, they should be empathic to the trying day she has had and should not be surprised if her panic symptoms are worse than they were the day prior.

4. Make plans for the week regarding what exposures the adolescent is going to conduct with her parents. Particularly for older teens, or those for whom the parents are safety objects, design some reasonable exposures for the teen to conduct alone. Help the family create a reasonable, but challenging, schedule for exposures and emphasize rewarding the adolescent's accomplishments.

5. At the end of Session 10, discuss and provide parents with Parent Handout #5: You and Your Less Anxious Teen, which addresses the inevitable change of having a nonanxious (or less anxious) teen (e.g., teen might test limits more, be less attached, and more independent, etc.).

Chapter 12 | *Session 11: Relapse Prevention and Therapy Termination*

(Corresponds to chapter 8 of the workbook)

Materials Needed

- Copy of adolescent's Fear and Avoidance Hierarchy (FAH) form
- Blank copy of Fear and Avoidance Hierarchy (FAH) form
- Copy of adolescent's My Goals form
- Taking Stock of All You've Accomplished form
- Becoming Your Own Therapist form
- Weighing My Options form (optional)
- Planning Ahead form

Outline

- Review homework exposures
- Re-rate FAH form
- Revisit treatment goals and accomplishments
- Help adolescent develop a practice plan
- Assess the cost of improvement
- Prepare the adolescent for symptom fluctuations
- Plan for symptom increases
- Terminate therapy
- Conduct optional parent component

Homework Review

Review the final homework exposures completed by the patient and congratulate him on his accomplishments. If the patient had problems, review them and how he handled them, and provide corrective feedback as appropriate. Assist the patient to use his experiences (both successes and failures) as evidence to challenge anxious thoughts and catastrophic predictions.

Re-rating Fear and Avoidance Hierarchy

Review the patient's FAH and have him re-rate the fear and avoidance ratings for each situation. Encourage the patient to notice improvements in fear and avoidance ratings after treatment. In addition, encourage patient to engage in self-praise for his accomplishments.

Revisiting Treatment Goals and Accomplishments

Review the patient's My Goals form completed in the first session. Identify which goals have been achieved and which ones still need more work.

Discuss with the patient the Taking Stock of All You've Accomplished form found in the workbook. Help the patient fill out this form by pointing out his strengths and accomplishments.

Developing a Practice Plan

Using the patient's re-ratings on his FAH and the other information obtained during the session, assist the patient to develop a list of assignments to do during the next month, focusing on areas of residual problems most in need of work. If several areas are in need of work, the plan should address them roughly in proportion to their relative importance. Use the Becoming Your Own Therapist form in the workbook to develop this plan. You may also help the adolescent create a new FAH if needed.

Let the patient take the lead in developing the plan, emphasizing the need to become his own therapist. You might begin by asking the patient to suggest the plan, based on your discussions in the session.

The tasks to be done should be specified in detail. Therapists often fail to do this. It is not sufficient to tell the patient to continue to work on cognitive restructuring or interoceptive or situational exposures. Specify what thoughts are to be restructured or what specific activities the patient is to engage in, how often, and for how long. Unless assignments are specific, the patient may choose tasks that are not sufficiently challenging. Also, he will be more likely to do assignments if they are specific.

Encourage the patient to schedule specific times for practices. Just as it helps to schedule specific times to go to the gym or health club if one is working on a fitness program, it is important to schedule specific times to exercise panic skills. Otherwise, practices likely won't get done. Practicing skills repeatedly in real-life situations is the most important and essential part of treatment. The more often the patient practices, the better.

Encourage the patient to review and update his practice plan every month.

Assessing the Cost of Improvement

In this section, your goal is to assist the patient to:

1. Identify costs of improvement that could undermine his recovery

2. Weigh those costs against the benefits of improvement

3. Make a conscious decision to pay the costs

Explain that costs like these, of which the patient may not be consciously aware, can undermine recovery and affect his motivation to improve. It is important to consider them. Ask the patient if any costs like these pertain to him, or if he can think of any other costs his improvement could entail. You may want to use the Weighing My Options form from Session 1.

If the patient identifies any costs of improvement, ask him to weigh those against the benefits of completely overcoming his anxiety and avoidance (e.g., can do things that he couldn't do before, has more confidence, etc.) and decide if he is willing to pay them. If so, encourage the patient to commit himself to accomplishing his treatment goals. If not, you might further explore why with the patient, as getting better from panic disorder (PD) is so important to him.

Preparing for Symptom Fluctuations

The therapist goals for this portion of the session are:

▪ To identify and assist the patient to restructure any unrealistic thoughts he has about the experience of symptoms in the future

▪ To distinguish among expected symptom fluctuations, a lapse, and a relapse

▪ To decatastrophize symptom increases

▪ To help the patient to begin working on a plan for coping with symptom increases

Encouraging Appropriate Expectations

Attempt to identify any unrealistic or worrisome thoughts the patient has about the extent or durability of his improvement in the months ahead. Start by asking the patient open-ended questions such as:

▪ *How do you think things will go in the next several months?*

▪ *How confident are you that you will be able to maintain or extend your improvement?*

▪ *Do you anticipate any difficulties?*

The thoughts you are looking for fall into two broad categories:

1. Unrealistically optimistic expectations (e.g., never have another panic attack; never be anxious in situations again; no setbacks)

2. Worry about relapsing (e.g., lack of confidence about managing anxiety or panic; expectation that minor stress could undo all of

his gains; belief that he will have to struggle with anxiety the rest of his life)

Challenge or normalize the patient's thoughts, as appropriate. If he has unrealistically optimistic expectations, commend him on his confidence and accomplishments during treatment, but point out that the best way to ensure success is to anticipate and prepare for setbacks. Anxiety is strongly influenced by situational events, and possibly also by internal factors (e.g., hormones, illness). If a patient does not allow for that, the occurrence of a panic attack in the future, or even of normal anxiety symptoms, could be misinterpreted catastrophically (e.g., as a failure of treatment). Even if that isn't the case, the patient will be less able to manage if he has not kept his skills sharp.

If the patient has worries about relapsing, tell him that this is normal at this point in treatment. Treatment has been short and has covered a lot of material. Patients usually are not confident in the skills they have learned or worry that without further contact with the therapist, they will slip back. Remind the patient that he now owns his skills and has already applied them on his own without therapist assistance.

Symptom Fluctuation, Lapse, and Relapse

First explain that anxiety and panic symptoms typically fluctuate over time. This is the normal course of events. Times when symptoms are likely to increase include:

Periods of stress. Anxiety and panic attacks often begin during a period of stress, and increases in stress can make them worse. Stressful times require more skill and effort to maintain improvement and are times when symptom breakthroughs or increases are more likely to occur. School problems, dating conflicts, disagreements with friends, parental discord—all are times of increased risk. Positive events, like moving to a new home, taking a long-avoided trip, going back to school, dating a new person, or starting a new job, although exciting, also can be sources of stress.

During illness or as an effect of medications. Aside from being stressful in general, illnesses have the added dimension of causing anxiety-related symptoms of their own. Some illnesses cause symptoms the patient may associate with panic or anxiety (e.g., a cold can cause chest tightness and breathlessness; an ear infection, dizziness; the flu, weakness and hot flushes). In addition, some medications (e.g., decongestants) and substances like caffeine have stimulating effects that may cause sensations like anxiety.

Next distinguish among: (1) expected normal symptom fluctuations, (2) a lapse or setback, and (3) a relapse.

Therapist Note

■ *The boundaries between these three categories of symptom increases are not clearly defined, but it is useful for patients to conceptualize them as distinct, because they have different implications.* ■

Expected Symptom Fluctuations

Everyone feels anxious sometimes, and about 30% of the population experience occasional panic attacks. People who have had PD clearly are in that 30%. The experience of anxiety during stressful periods, and even occasional panic attacks, are therefore normal and, provided the patient does not misinterpret or overreact to them, are not reasons for concern.

In addition, patients who make it to maintenance therapy may have residual maladaptive thoughts and behaviors that give rise to symptom fluctuations that are greater than most people experience. Such symptoms (e.g., in agoraphobic situations or in response to physical sensations) are expected for the patient and do not represent a loss of improvement unless their severity increases over time. Rather than label them as lapses, conceptualize them as indicators of those areas in need of further work during maintenance therapy.

Lapse or Setback

In contrast to expected symptom fluctuations, a "lapse" is a slip or partial loss of improvement. Lapses must be distinguished from the background of expected fluctuations for a given patient and may be conceptualized as increases in symptoms *beyond expected fluctuations* or an increase in avoidance or functional impairment due to panic-related concerns. In judging these, both intensity and time should be considered. For example, the experience of a panic attack, even if unprovoked or severe, may not constitute a lapse if the patient successfully coped with it (in this case, the attack could be described as an expected or common occurrence in people with PD, which the patient handled well). On the other hand, a small increase in agoraphobic anxiety or avoidance that persists or grows over time would represent a lapse.

Lapses may be due to situational or internal stressors or may simply be due to lack of practice of anxiety management skills. It is hard to stick to a diet or exercise program, especially when things are going well. Just as pounds can creep back on when a person cheats on a diet, symptoms can reemerge when the patient neglects practicing coping skills. Lapses should be viewed as signs that increased effort is needed to sharpen skills. Recognizing symptoms and sharpening skills promptly may prevent a lapse from turning into a relapse.

Relapse

Finally, a "relapse" is conceptualized as a full and persistent return of symptoms or avoidance to pretreatment levels or higher. Again, relapses typically begin as lapses that are not addressed and can be prevented if the patient applies effective coping strategies in high-risk situations and when lapses occur.

Decatastrophizing Symptom Increases

Explain that symptom fluctuations, and even occasional lapses, are common and should be anticipated, just as getting out of shape physically, putting pounds back on after a diet, and breaking New Year's resolutions happen. If the patient misinterprets such events as a relapse, he may become discouraged or hopeless, blame himself, or think that treatment has failed. To prevent that, it is important to keep symptom increases in perspective. When they occur, catastrophic thoughts about them should be handled using the cognitive countering techniques learned during treatment. Encourage the patient to view symptom increases as reminders as well as opportunities to practice and sharpen skills that he learned during treatment.

Planning for Symptom Increases

Assist the patient to begin working on a plan for coping with symptom increases. The goal of this section is to help the patient think like a therapist when confronted with an increase in symptoms or a situation that may put the patient at increased risk for slips. By now, he should be able to evaluate increases in anxiety within the three-component model (i.e., assess separately for increases in scary sensations, anxious thoughts, and avoidance or safety behaviors) and to identify the appropriate interventions for each component (i.e., interoceptive exposure, cognitive countering, situational exposure).

This section should be completed using Socratic questioning techniques (that is, instead of telling the patient, ask him what interventions would be appropriate). The following statement can be used to begin:

> *Because your symptoms are likely to increase from time to time, it is important to anticipate that and have a plan for how to respond. The earlier and more aggressive the response, the more likely the increases can be nipped in the bud.*

Direct the patient's attention to the Planning Ahead form in the workbook and ask him what situations or stressful events might occur in the next several months (or longer) that that could possibly cause an increase or lapse in panic symptoms. Have the patient write down any he can think of on the form.

Remind the patient that the anxiety management skills he has learned are directed toward the three different components of anxiety. Accordingly, the most appropriate intervention(s) to use in the event of an increase in anxiety will depend what is increasing. The Planning Ahead form includes examples of possible symptom increases and strategies for the situation of going on a school field trip.

Ask the patient what form he thinks a lapse might take in his case, if it were to occur. Specifically, what anxious thoughts might return, what sensations might again begin to scare him, and what avoidance or safety behaviors might creep back. Have him write these in the corresponding cells of the Planning Ahead form.

Using the examples provided on the Planning Ahead form as a guide, ask the patient what strategies he could use to address each of the slips he predicted. Have the patient be as specific as possible. Note that strategies such as cutting down on caffeine, taking medication, seeking or giving oneself simple reassurance, avoiding stressful situations, doing controlled breathing or relaxation exercises, and the like are not acceptable, as they only function to make the anxiety more intense in the long run.

Instruct the patient to work on expanding and refining his plan during the next week. Finally, tell the patient that working on the plan is an important step in preparing for symptom increases, but even more important is being able to implement it when it is needed. To help with that, say you would like the patient to *rehearse* implementing it. To rehearse, he should imagine as vividly as possible that he has experienced (preferably in a real risk situation) a lapse of the predicted thoughts, symptoms, and behaviors and then imagine himself carrying out the planned interventions and regaining control. He should do this frequently during the next month.

Terminate Therapy

At the end of the session, congratulate the patient on completing the treatment. Praise him for his accomplishments and acknowledge the efforts he made. Be sure to tell the patient that it has been a pleasure working with him and that you are confident that he will continue to do well.

If the patient asks if he can call you if problems arise, say that if he feels unable to handle a situation on his own, he is welcome to call. However, you are confident he can handle almost anything if he trusts in the skills he has learned. It is time now for him to be his own therapist. You may want to schedule a few follow-up phone calls to check on the patient's progress.

Respond to any other termination questions as appropriate and say your goodbyes. Sometimes, with younger adolescents, therapists might consider creating a "bravery certificate" or "certificate of accomplishment" for the adolescent to take home.

Optional Parent Component

Parent(s)/caregiver(s) join the adolescent for the final 10–15 minutes of the session. Use the following agenda:

1. Ask parents to tell their child some of the things he did during the past week that they are most proud of. Ask the adolescent to state some of the things he is most proud of that occurred during the week as well.

2. Have the adolescent teach his parents (with therapist assistance as needed) about the following:
   a. difference between lapse and relapse
   b. why lapses/relapses occur
   c. how to prevent them
   d. any costs associated with improvement

3. Share with the parents the Becoming Your Own Therapist and Planning Ahead forms that were completed during session with the adolescent. Get parental feedback about feasibility, other things to add, and so forth. Discuss any potential "roadblocks" to the adolescent continuing to make progress with practicing exposures.

4. Discuss openly the ways that family roles might change as the adolescent continues to get better and becomes more active in his life with peers, school, and the like. Ask parents to provide their perspective on ways they anticipate that family life will improve now that the adolescent is feeling better, and also ask the adolescent to discuss his views of this issue.

Chapter 13 *Adaptation*

The first two sections of this chapter provide information on adapting the regular program for different ages and for patients with asthma. The rest of the chapter outlines the adaptation for the intensive treatment program.

Adapting for Different Ages

When implementing any psychological treatment, it is important to consider the developmental level of the child or adolescent when introducing skills and new materials. Although the chronological age of the child is significant, the child's developmental age or maturity is most important. For example, much variability exists in the cognitive abilities, maturity, and levels of independence among 12-year-olds. A young, less mature adolescent (developmental age of 11 or 12) may need to have skills written out very clearly, in a "step-by-step" fashion, or may need to have the therapist give him many concrete examples of how to utilize the tools learned in therapy. For example, when teaching cognitive restructuring, younger adolescents still might benefit from and enjoy the idea of being a "detective" with their own thoughts, or might benefit highly from having the therapist work with them to restructure *several* maladaptive thoughts before doing one on their own. In addition, it is important that the therapist be sensitive about not using language or terms that might be unfamiliar to a younger adolescent. For that reason, when working with a younger adolescent, the therapist might use the term "worry thoughts" instead of "maladaptive thoughts," whereas the language used with a 17-year-old might be more sophisticated.

The developmental level of the adolescent becomes even more important to keep in mind when conducting exposure exercises. Although the therapist should remove "safety behaviors," she should keep in mind the overall safety of the young adolescent and think of exposures that do not jeopardize the patient. For example, the therapist should avoid exposures that require leaving a young adolescent alone in an unfamiliar neighborhood, or that require that a developmentally immature adolescent be able to read train or bus schedules alone and find the right transportation back to the office. Although this latter exposure may be within the ability level of most older adolescents, a younger adolescent might have difficulty with it, and it may not be safe or appropriate to have the adolescent travel alone. Thus, the therapist should brainstorm some possible exposures that are part of the adolescent's hierarchy, but are places and activities that the parent and therapist agree would be acceptable and generally safe.

The treatment also may be adapted for patients as young as 9 years old with appropriate language adaptations and with therapist accompaniment on exposures (e.g., using public transportation, etc.).

Adaptations for Asthma

Adolescents with both asthma and panic disorder (PD) are often very in tune with interoceptive cues regarding breathing. In some cases, these adolescents might be hypersensitive to any changes in their breathing, even when they are not having an asthma attack. The elevated heart rate and rapid breathing that typically accompany a panic attack can trigger a cycle of worry regarding whether the adolescent can breathe, lead to overuse of an inhaler, and lead to worry and confusion regarding whether the adolescent is actually experiencing a panic attack, an asthma attack, or both.

When working with adolescents with asthma, the therapist should be sure to carefully delineate as part of the three-component model those "triggers" that often induce asthma (such as an allergy, temperature change, exercise, etc.) and encourage the adolescent to take the inhaler as prescribed during these situations. Use of the common asthma medication albuterol also naturally increases one's heart rate, which can lead to further worry regarding whether or not a panic attack will occur. Therapists might outline a "cycle of asthma" that looks similar to the three-circle model "cycle of panic" and highlight some of the differences in the triggers for asthma and the triggers for panic. This might help the adolescent distinguish better between them. Also, when conducting exposures, adolescents with asthma might worry that a panic attack might induce an asthma attack. We recommend getting a doctor's approval for asthmatic adolescents' participation in treatment, along with formulating a clear plan for therapists and adolescents to follow if an asthma attack does occur during treatment. Some practitioners suggest using an inhaler prior to going out on exposures, so that the adolescent does not have to worry about the onset of asthma, but can focus solely on the panic attacks. In any case, the therapist can let the adolescent know that, in some ways, having asthma has helped him become very in tune with interoceptive cues. When having a panic attack, these adolescents might be very skilled at noticing even minute changes in their bodily state, which can help them learn more about the nature of their panic attacks.

Intensive Treatment

Pincus, et al. (2003) recently conducted a pilot study to determine the efficacy of an 8-day intensive treatment of panic disorder and agoraphobia that was developmentally adapted for use with adolescents. Intensive Panic Control Treatment for Adolescent Panic Disorder and Agoraphobia (APE) was modeled after a similar program for adults developed by David Spiegel and David Barlow (Spiegel & Barlow, 2000).

The intensive program is intended to treat patients with panic disorder with the full range of agoraphobic avoidance (PDA). It is conducted over 8 consecutive days and incorporates a self-study format combined with therapist guidance. Rather than following a hierarchically based exposure plan, interoceptive and situational exposures are conducted in an ungraded massed fashion. Furthermore, the exposure aspect of treatment is particularly unique in that it emphasizes the deliberate provocation and maximal intensification of anxious symptoms without teaching any arousal reduction procedures. Other aspects of Panic Control Treatment (PCT), particularly psychoeducation and cognitive restructuring, are also part of the treatment (Spiegel & Barlow, 2000; Heinrichs, Spiegel, & Hofmann, 2002).

The primary objective of the pilot study (Pincus et al., 2003) was to assess the impact of the 8-day APE on the clinical symptoms of PDA, and on the overall quality of life of adolescents. Eighteen adolescents (12 girls, six boys) between the ages of 12 and 17 (mean age, 14.5 years) were included. Thirteen out of the eighteen families were from states other than Massachusetts, and five were from the local Boston area. These five families specifically asked for a more "intensive" form of therapy. Families from outside the local Boston area traveled to Boston and stayed in lodgings in close proximity to the Center for Anxiety and Related Disorders (CARD) for the duration of the 8-day treatment program. Adolescents and their parents were all administered the Anxiety Disorders Interview Schedule for the DSM-IV, Child and Parent Versions (ADIS-IV-C/P) (Silverman & Albano, 1997) at pretreatment, posttreatment, and at 1 and 3 months' follow-up. At pretreatment, 12 adolescents attended school regularly, whereas six refused to attend school due to fears of having panic attacks in the classroom. In addition, at pretreatment assessment, the adolescents reported having an average of 11.4 panic attacks per week, and reported experiencing distress and interference in several areas of their lives. At pretreatment, all adolescents were given clinician severity ratings on the ADIS-IV-C/P above the clinical level, ranging from 5–7. No significant differences were found at pretreatment between those from the local Boston area and those from out of town on any demographic variables or on pretreatment self-report or parent report measures.

APE was administered to patients over 8 consecutive days. Adolescents and parents were provided with self-study reading material each evening, and the therapist reviewed and clarified material during sessions. In the first 3 days of treatment, adolescents learned about the nature of anxiety and panic, including the physiology of anxiety, and were taught skills such as cognitive restructuring and hypothesis testing. They also learned how to create a personalized Fear and Avoidance Hierarchy (FAH) and were taught the concepts of exposure and habituation. These first three sessions lasted approximately 2–3 hours each. Adolescents met individually with the therapist, and parents were included in the last half hour of the session to teach them the skills the adolescents had learned. Adolescents and parents were taught skills such as acknowledging the "cycle of panic," cognitive restructuring, recognizing avoidance and safety behaviors, and practicing interoceptive exercises. During days 4–7 of treatment, adolescents participated in situational exposures with integrated interoceptive exposure exercises for 5–7 hours per day (2 days with therapist accompaniment, 2 days with family accompaniment). The therapist taught the adolescents and parents how to conduct interoceptive and situational exposures, and then assisted them in entering situations listed on the adolescents' FAH. During day 8 of treatment, adolescents met with the therapist for approximately 2 hours to learn skills to prevent relapse, discuss ways to maintain gains, and plan future self-directed exposure sessions. Parents were included in the last half of this session for an open discussion of these issues with their child with therapist mediation.

Results of this pilot study indicated that the clinical severity ratings (CSR) of PD (based on the ADIS-IV-C/P) significantly decreased from pre- to posttreatment, with 14 out of 18 adolescents displaying nonclinical levels of PD by posttreatment. Because of more substantial agoraphobia, this was a more severe group than in our ongoing 11-week study. Follow-up clinician severity ratings at 1 and 3 months posttreatment indicated that the adolescents' gains were maintained at each follow-up point. At 1 month posttreatment, 17 out of 18 adolescents received nonclinical CSRs for PDA, and reported that panic was no longer significantly interfering in their lives.

At 1 month following treatment, adolescents reported a mean of 2.2 panic attacks per week, as compared to 11.4 at pretreatment (self-monitoring of weekly panic attacks obviously is not recorded at posttreatment, as that would include the week of treatment). At 3 months follow-up, the number of reported panic attacks was further decreased to an average of 1.5 per week. Adolescents' anxiety sensitivity, as measured by the Childhood Anxiety Sensitivity Index (CASI), decreased from pre- to posttreatment, and was maintained at follow-up points.

Numerous collateral changes were also reported by families, including improved academic performance, improved social functioning, and improved family functioning. Adolescents reported decreased depression and avoidance of situations due to panic. Parents reported feeling more knowledgeable about the factors that cause and maintain panic and reported feeling more confident in their abilities to effectively deal with adolescents during a panic attack. They also reported improved interactions with their adolescents, as they utilized skills learned in therapy to positively encourage their children's nonavoidance of previously avoided situations. Changes in parents' perceptions of their adolescents' overall adjustment also improved, as evidenced by decreased scores on the Child Behavior Checklist.

Based on the positive results of this pilot study, a randomized controlled trial of intensive treatment for PDA in adolescence is currently underway (NIMH: Pincus, PI). The aims of the study are to investigate the efficacy of an intensive treatment program for treating panic and agoraphobia in adolescents, to evaluate the relative advantages of involving parents in treatment, and to examine mechanisms of action in treatment. Thus far, approximately 30 adolescents have been treated with intensive treatment, and initial results are quite positive. Adolescents have shown decreases in their overall clinical severity of panic, decreases in the frequency of panic attacks, and numerous positive collateral changes.

Benefits

Although an 11-week version of PCT has been shown to be initially efficacious (Mattis, Pincus, Ehrenreich, & Barlow, under review), there are many reasons why an intensive treatment option may be very attractive to families of adolescents with PDA. First, many adolescents with PDA show significant interference in developmentally appropriate activities, and approximately half do not attend school regularly. Intensive treatment can help adolescents return to normal daily functioning rather quickly, which may make it especially appropriate for adolescents who are not attending school or for those who attend school but experience significant distress. Second, for those families who do not have access to appropriate forms of treatment near their hometowns, the option of on-site 1-week intensive treatment may be ideal. Third, intensive treatment might be especially useful for those adolescents with PDA who have tried other therapies without success. Some adolescents benefit greatly from the therapist-accompanied in vivo exposure time that an intensive form of therapy offers. In sum, many families of adolescents with PDA find it favorable to have treatment intensified into 8 days, rather than stretching therapy out over the course of several months.

Another benefit to conducting treatment intensively is that the therapist and patient have a short but "intense" period of time in which to build rapport and work on skills. Rather than losing ground over weeks and months of therapy (due to missed sessions, etc.), the intensive treatment format allows the therapist to keep the patient motivated to make changes. Often, the result is quite positive, and patients often leave the intensive program feeling as if their lives have been "changed in 8 days." Parents also describe that they feel the intensive nature of the program is extremely helpful and that it gives adolescents "their lives back."

One drawback to intensive format of treatment, however, is that less time is available to follow up with adolescents over time, especially if the patient is from out of town. It is important to be sure that the adolescent has a follow-up therapist in her home town, if necessary, to ensure adequate maintenance of skills. Also, because of the short time period of treatment, less time is available to deal with issues regarding adolescents who do not comply or who are not motivated to try.

Notes to Therapist

To conduct intensive treatment, the therapist must have solid training in PCT for adolescents, cognitive-behavioral principles, and treating adolescents. Furthermore, therapists need to prepare themselves for having to motivate an adolescent who has been avoiding developmentally appropriate activities for a long time. Often, parents have inadvertently developed maladaptive ways of helping their child, and this only further perpetuates the child's dependence on his parents. The therapist should have an awareness of these family dynamics in order to effect lasting change on the adolescent and his family system.

Schedule

Treatment must be scheduled for a week when the patient can devote full time (at least 8 hours per day) to therapy for 8 consecutive days. That may require families to take time off work or school, arrange for child-care, and obtain the cooperation of family members. The therapist must emphasize the importance of this and ensure that the family has made adequate arrangements to protect the allotted time. In this regard, the treatment can be compared to an 8-day hospitalization.

Session Frequency and Duration

APE is administered over an 8-day period, as depicted in Table 13.1. These session numbers correspond to the sessions of this manual; how-ever, during intensive treatment, more than one session may be covered per meeting. Generally, sessions 1 through 7 are conducted Monday through Friday, sessions 8 to 10 are completed by the patient over the weekend, and the final session is held on the following Monday. Every effort should be made to adhere to this schedule; however, if necessary to accommodate unavoidable interruptions, sessions may be delayed or rescheduled. It is recommended, however, that the entire treatment be completed within a maximum of 12 days.

On treatment days 1–3 and 8, the therapist typically meets with the patient for 2 hours to cover the session material. The duration of sessions 6 and 7 on days 4 and 5 will depend upon the nature of the exposures to be done and the rapidity and practicality with which therapist accompaniment can be faded. In preliminary studies, therapist involvement in these two sessions combined averaged approximately 10 hours.

Table 13.1 Outline of Sessions

Treatment Day(s)	Corresponds to Sessions	Treatment Component
1–3	1–5	Cognitive-behavioral therapy and interoceptive exposure
4, 5	6–7	Intensive situational exposure with initial therapist accompaniment
6, 7	8–10	Continued exposure, patient working independently or with family members
8	11	Skill consolidation and relapse prevention

Scheduled Posttreatment Contacts

It is recommended that therapists contact patients at several points after the conclusion of treatment (e.g., once a week). These contacts will generally be made by telephone and should not exceed 30 minutes each. The purpose is to provide a transitional end to therapy, assess for possible deterioration that might require intervention, and provide a context for discontinuation of pharmacotherapy. After the intensely emotional experience of the 8-day treatment, it seems unnatural to abruptly terminate treatment and not have any further contact. It is also possible that a patient might be reluctant to report a lapse, so that leaving contacts to the patient's initiative could result in deterioration going undetected until the follow-up assessment. The addition of regular contact will systematize posttreatment interactions and ensure closer monitoring of patient status.

Exposures

In the intensive treatment, exposure are conducted over four days (days 4–7), with the last 2 days usually occurring over a weekend in which the patient practices exposures on her own. At the end of the third day, the therapist explains to the patient that the next four days are the most important days of treatment, the days for which they have been preparing and during which the greatest gains will be made. During the next few days, the patient will face some of the most difficult situations that can be arranged and will need to do this for about 8 hours per day. It will be hard, but it will also be short, and the therapist will be there to guide and assist the patient. The following dialogue may be used:

> *Just as a surgeon does not scratch at the surface but goes quickly to the site of the problem, so we will go quickly to the most difficult of your situations. This is a much more powerful method than gradual exposure over weeks or months and will get the discomfort over much sooner. People literally can change their lives dramatically within a few days.*
>
> *Also like surgery, exposure therapy requires informed consent. You can choose to keep a cancerous organ or live a life restricted by fear, or you*

can choose to courageously endure 4 days of pain and discomfort in order to break the back of panic disorder and recover your health and freedom. We are providing a unique opportunity, one you are not likely to have again, but you must decide for yourself whether the benefit is worth the cost.

See Chapter 9 on how to handle common patient objections to doing exposures. In addition, if the patient acknowledges the need to do exposure but gives excuses for not going ahead with it now (e.g., something has come up, under unusual stress at the moment, anxious because of coming off medication, dealing with withdrawal symptoms, not feeling well physically), the therapist can point out that it is now or never for this program. The therapist has set aside the next 2 days to work with the patient.

If the patient agrees to go forward at the end of the third day, the therapist should encourage her to start exposures on her own that night or the next morning, if she feels able to (e.g., taking public transportation home or to the clinic, taking an elevator, etc.).

Prior to day 4, the therapist should give some thought to the exposures to be done. From review of the patient's pretreatment ADIS and the preceding CBT sessions, the therapist should by this point have a good idea of tasks that would be appropriate. Some of these may require advance planning (e.g., checking schedules, deciding on the need for a car, getting directions or a map). If so, that should be done before day 4, so as not to lose time in session. The plans will be refined, and possibly changed, when the therapist meets with the patient in the morning to go over her fear and avoidance hierarchy, so the therapist should allow for flexibility. Tasks that need firm schedules (e.g., appointments or reservations) are best done during the second day of exposures, after the therapist sees how well the patient does.

Day 4 (session 6) begins in the office, to discuss the rationale for exposure, deal with patient resistance, and complete the FAH form. After that, the therapist and patient go to wherever the exposures are to be done. No specific time limits need be set for this session, but the patient should spend most of the day (at least 6 hours) doing exposures. The therapist should fade her presence out as the day proceeds.

Appendix A | *Panic Disorder Severity Scale for Adolescents (PDSS-A)*

Panic Disorder Severity Scale for Adolescents (PDSS-A)[1]

Date: _____ Name: _____

Instructions. Several of the following questions refer to panic attacks and limited symptom attacks. For this questionnaire, a *panic attack* is defined as a *sudden rush* of fear or discomfort accompanied by *at least four of the symptoms listed below*. In order to qualify as a sudden rush, the symptoms must *peak within 10 minutes*. Episodes like panic attacks but having fewer than four of the listed symptoms are called *limited-symptom attacks*. Here are the symptoms to count:

- Rapid or pounding heartbeat
- Sweating
- Trembling or shaking
- Breathlessness

- Feeling of choking
- Chest pain or discomfort
- Nausea
- Dizziness or faintness
- Feelings of unreality

- Numbness or tingling
- Chills or hot flushes
- Fear of losing control or going crazy
- Fear of dying

For each question below, circle the number of the answer that best describes your experience during the *past week*.

1. How many panic and limited-symptoms attacks did you have during the past week?
   - 0 — No panic or limited-symptom episodes
   - 1 — Mild: No full panic attacks and no more than one limited-symptom attack per day
   - 2 — Moderate: One or two full panic attacks and/or multiple limited-symptom attacks per day
   - 3 — Severe: More than two full attacks but not more than one per day on average
   - 4 — Extreme: Full panic attacks occurred more than once a day, more days than not

2. If you had any panic attacks during the past week, how distressing (uncomfortable, frightening) were they *while they were happening*? (If you had more than one, give an average rating. If you didn't have any panic attacks but did have limited-symptom attacks, answer for the limited-symptom attacks.)
   - 0 — Not at all distressing, or no panic or limited-symptom attacks during the past week
   - 1 — Mildly distressing (not too intense)
   - 2 — Moderately distressing (intense, but still manageable)
   - 3 — Severely distressing (very intense)
   - 4 — Extremely distressing (extreme distress during all attacks)

3. During the past week, how much have you worried or felt anxious *about when your next panic attack would occur, or about fears related to the attacks* (for example, that they could mean you have physical or mental health problems or could cause you social embarrassment)?
   - 0 — Not at all
   - 1 — Occasionally or only mildly
   - 2 — Frequently or moderately
   - 3 — Very often or to a very disturbing degree
   - 4 — Nearly constantly and to a disabling extent

[1]Modified by D. A. Spiegel and M. K. Shear from an interview-based version published by Shear et al. in 1997.

4. During the past week, were there any *places or situations* (e.g., public transportation, movie theaters, crowds, bridges, tunnels, shopping malls, being alone) you avoided, or felt afraid of (uncomfortable in, wanted to avoid or leave), *because of fear of having a panic attack*? Are there any other situations that you would have avoided or been afraid of if they had come up during the week, for the same reason? If yes to either question, please rate your level of fear and avoidance this past week.

   0 — None: No fear or avoidance

   1 — Mild: Occasional fear and/or avoidance, but I could usually confront or endure the situation. There was little or no modification of my lifestyle due to this.

   2 — Moderate: Noticeable fear and/or avoidance, but still manageable. I avoided some situations but I could confront them with a companion. There was some modification of my lifestyle because of this, but my overall functioning was not impaired.

   3 — Severe: Extensive avoidance. Substantial modification of my lifestyle was required to accommodate the avoidance, making it difficult to manage usual activities.

   4 — Extreme: Pervasive disabling fear and/or avoidance. Extensive modification in my lifestyle was required, such that important tasks were not performed.

5. During the past week, were there any *activities* (e.g., physical exertion, taking a hot shower or bath, drinking coffee, watching an exciting or scary movie) that you avoided, or felt afraid of (uncomfortable doing, wanted to avoid or stop), *because they caused physical sensations like those you feel during panic attacks or that you were afraid might trigger a panic attack*? Are there any other activities that you would have avoided or been afraid of if they had come up during the week, for that reason? If yes to either question, please rate your level of fear and avoidance of those activities this past week.

   0 — No fear or avoidance of situations or activities because of distressing physical sensations

   1 — Mild: Occasional fear and/or avoidance, but usually I could confront or endure with little distress activities that cause physical sensations. There was little modification of my lifestyle due to this.

   2 — Moderate: Noticeable avoidance, but still manageable. There was definite, but limited, modification of my lifestyle, such that my overall functioning was not impaired.

   3 — Severe: Extensive avoidance. There was substantial modification of my lifestyle or interference in my functioning.

   4 — Extreme: Pervasive and disabling avoidance. There was extensive modification in my lifestyle due to this, such that important tasks or activities were not performed.

6. During the past week, how much did the above symptoms altogether (panic and limited-symptom attacks, worry about attacks, and fear of situations and activities because of attacks) interfere with your *ability to work, go to school, or carry out your responsibilities at home*? (If your work or home responsibilities were less than usual this past week, answer how you think you would have done if the responsibilities had been usual.)

   0 — No interference with work or home responsibilities.

   1 — Slight interference with work or home responsibilities, but I could do nearly everything I could do if I didn't have these problems.

   2 — Significant interference with work or home responsibilities, but I still could manage to do the things I needed to do.

3 — Substantial impairment in work or home responsibilities; there were many important things I couldn't do because of these problems.

4 — Extreme, incapacitating impairment, such that I was essentially unable to manage any work or home responsibilities.

7. During the past week, how much did panic and limited-symptom attacks, worry about attacks, and fear of situations and activities because of attacks, interfere with your *social life*? (If you didn't have many opportunities to socialize this past week, answer how you think you would have done if you did have opportunities.)

0 — No interference.

1 — Slight interference with social activities, but I could do nearly everything I could do if I didn't have these problems.

2 — Significant interference with social activities, but I could manage to do most things if I made the effort.

3 — Substantial impairment in social activities; there were many social things I couldn't do because of these problems.

4 — Extreme, incapacitating impairment, such that there was hardly anything social I could do.

Your Score (add the seven numbers you circled) _____

Appendix B *Parent Handouts*

Parent Handout #1
Parenting Anxious Youth: 101

The Pusher

You just need to go. We're going now, and you have to go with us. You used to go all the time, you can go now.

Why you do it:

Because you've seen your child become more isolated from the world, and you're concerned. You've seen your child hold back from doing things, either from things she has done before or from things that her siblings and friends are doing. You feel that, if you could just get her to go, she would enjoy it once she got there and realize that it's not as scary as she thinks.

What's good about it:

Ultimately, we do want your child to do the things that make her anxious and face her fears.

Why it doesn't work:

It can feel invalidating to the child, as if you do not understand how anxious, upset, or uncomfortable this situation makes her. Also, your child does not, yet, have the skills necessary to handle those anxious, uncomfortable feelings. It is likely that, even if you do succeed in getting her to approach the situation, she will "fail," either by panicking or otherwise feeling overwhelmed by the situation. She will then decide that she was right all along—she can't handle the situation, and it is too scary.

The Softy

What's the matter, honey? Your heart is racing and you feel sick to your stomach? OK, if going to school (or Sam's party or soccer tryouts) is this hard, maybe you should just stay home.

Why you do it:

One of the most basic instincts of parenting is to keep your child safe from harm. When a child is upset, hurt, or distraught, we want to fix it, by whatever means necessary. Often parents worry about making their child worse by pushing her, sometimes even stating their concern about "traumatizing" their child by making her do something that is so obviously distressing.

What's good about it:

Often, a teen feels as if a parent who accedes to her fears is the one who "gets her"—the one who understands how real and significant her anxiety and distress truly is.

Why it doesn't work:

Avoidance is a pattern. Once it starts, it is hard to stop. The next time your child gets nervous before an event, she will think that the only tool for handling anxiety is to avoid it. Also, it sets up the idea that anxious feelings are bad, since you are trying to make them stop. Anxiety is a feeling; it is neither good nor bad, it is simply neutral. Just as you would never suggest that your child should never feel sad, angry, or frustrated, you would not want to suggest that she should never feel anxious. Finally, overreacting to the physical symptoms sends the message that these symptoms are dangerous. They are uncomfortable, to be certain, but not dangerous or harmful.

The Anticipator

Oh, boy. We just got this invitation from Aunt Jane to go to a family reunion. I know that 4 hours in the car is just too much for you. Plus, it's being held in a state park, so I'm not sure what the facilities will be like. I'll go ahead and decline.

Why you do it:

You know your child and her typical responses to these types of situations. You've already wasted time and money on unsuccessful ventures, whether they were family trips that had to be cancelled at the last minute or parties or other events that had to be left early, in the midst of panic. Rather than risk embarrassment for you and your child, it seems better just not to bother.

What's good about it:

Similar to "The Softy," your child may feel like you truly understand her since you can anticipate her feelings and limitations.

Why it doesn't work:

You are teaching your child that she can't do it and furthering her sense of "that's too hard for me to handle." You are modeling that things that make us anxious should be avoided, rather than faced. Also, you are setting up the idea that anxiety is embarrassing. The attitude that "we'd rather not go only to have to leave halfway through" suggests that your child should be embarrassed or ashamed of her anxiety problem.

The Importance of a United Front

Often parents differ in their approach to their child's anxiety—one might be "The Softy" while the other is "The Pusher." Teens are smart and savvy: they will pick up on this discrepancy quickly. Inconsistencies in parental responses can send mixed messages that can be confusing. It is important that whatever disagreements you and your spouse have behind the scenes, your child should think of you as a united front (not only about anxiety, but about all parenting decisions).

There is a healthy alternative to these ineffectual approaches:

The Ideal

I know you're not feeling well. This usually happens before a big test. Use the skills you've learned in therapy. I know it's hard, but I also know that you can do this. Think about how proud you are going to be of yourself when it's all over and you've done it. Let's think of a good reward— how about going out to dinner tomorrow?

Push compassionately:

Help your child push through the anxiety, and hold firm to expectations about her following through with the situation. But be equally sure to include empathy for the amount of distress the situation is causing her.

Focus on competency:

Reiterate (as many times as necessary) that your child has the ability to handle the situation. Help her to focus on the skills needed to complete the task rather than on the anxiety.

Downplay physical feelings:

Express compassion for the physical feelings, but no longer react to your child as you would if she were truly ill (e.g., if she had the stomach flu). Remind her that anxiety is causing the sensation, the sensation is time-limited (i.e., it won't last forever, it will end as soon as the anxiety does), and it is not harmful.

Be realistic:

If something is really hard (or perhaps is the first time the child is trying something new), keep the situation manageable in length and intensity, but with the understanding that each time the child tries it, she should push herself to stay a little longer.

Some of this may be different from your typical response to situations, and it may feel uncomfortable at first. Also, you may wonder why your other children have responded just fine to your usual interventions. It is important to note that your interventions weren't "bad parenting"; they simply were not the ideal way to handle a child with an anxious temperament. It is important to find a parenting style that fits with your child's temperament—since each child is different, your parenting may have to adjust slightly to best meet each child's needs.

Parent Handout #2
Behavioral Principles for Parenting Anxious Youth

Reinforcement

Positive reinforcement

Positive reinforcement is when a pleasant reward follows a behavior and tends to further encourage that behavior. As a parent, you want to positively reinforce those behaviors that you want to see continue. You also, however, must be careful not to reinforce those behaviors you want to stop. Think of a child having a tantrum in a grocery store: typically, the immediate response of a parent is to get the child to quiet down ASAP. Often this means leaving the store or giving the child a toy or a piece of candy to quiet down. These behaviors are rewarding for the child; therefore, he is likely to throw a tantrum the next time he gets upset in the grocery store.

You want to positively reinforce the behaviors you like (e.g., approaching anxiety-provoking situations) and be careful not to reinforce the behaviors you don't like (avoiding anxiety). While the obvious examples (like the tantrum) are easy to avoid, parents may often find themselves more subtly reinforcing behaviors that they do not like (e.g., allowing a child whose panic has kept him home from school that day to go out with his friends, thinking "Well, at least he is getting out of the house."). An example of using positive reinforcement appropriately is when your child goes to a previously avoided place or situation and you praise him for it, saying something like, "That's fantastic! I am so proud of the way you are learning not to avoid things!"

Human Slot Machine

The reason people play the slots is because they believe a chance exists that they might win big. That hope is fostered by the sounds of winning machines all around them and the fact that every once in a while, they, too, win some money. What makes playing the slots so irresistible is that it uses "variable reinforcement"—you never know if the next pull of the lever is the one that will win you the big money. If sometimes when your teen whines, gets upset, or panics he gets his way and other times he doesn't, you are a human slot machine. By varying in your response, your teen learns that if he keeps pushing, maybe the next tactic will be the one that will get "the big payoff" (i.e., the outcome he wants).

Even if you've been variable before, if you start being consistent now and continue to be consistent, eventually these behaviors will subside. This doesn't mean you can never be spontaneous or break from routine, it just means that first you have to create a culture of consistency, and then, when you are spontaneous or break from routine, it has to be on your terms and not on your teen's. So, once a consistent pattern has been set regarding curfew, for example, if you decide to extend his curfew because of a special event or as a treat for doing something good that week, this is a great reward and should be offered as such (e.g., "I am so proud of you! You worked so hard this week to face your anxiety, going to a mall and staying home by yourself for 2 hours, so I think you deserve an extra hour at curfew on Friday night."). However, extending curfew because you got tired of arguing about it reinforces the idea that your teen should argue with you in the future because eventually you might give up. Every time you give in, you reinforce the behavior of arguing.

Active Ignoring/Picking Your Battles

To avoid reinforcing negative behaviors, it is often advisable to ignore such behavior, unless it breaks a house rule, is dangerous to the teen (or to others), or is potentially harmful in some other way. This is called "active ignoring." You see the behavior, you don't approve of the behavior, but if it is not crossing an important line, you choose to ignore it. Thus, you refrain from subtly reinforcing the behavior (perhaps the teen is trying to get you to react), and you also minimize the number of negative interactions you have with your teen over the course of a day.

To further minimize arguments and increase the amount of positive interaction, it may be necessary to alter your expectations and "pick your battles." It is also important to pick your battles because, to avoid becoming a human slot machine, you do not want to set a limit or make a rule that you do not intend to enforce consistently.

Praise

All too often, especially with teens, parents fall into a trap of focusing on the negative. When teens are doing what they are expected to do (keeping their room clean, using good manners, getting their chores or homework done), little or no reinforcement is given for these behaviors. While this may work with many youth, teens with anxiety already tend to be hard on themselves and focus on the negative. As such, it's important to remember to praise them. Everyone likes to be praised, and praising acts as positive reinforcement. Remember, positively reinforced actions are more likely to continue. This goes for routine behaviors (e.g., emptying the dishwasher) as well as anxiety-related behaviors (e.g., going to a previously avoided place like the movie theater).

Labeled Praise

When giving your teen a compliment or praising him for something, be as specific as possible. So, when praising, be sure to reinforce the aspect of the behavior that you like (e.g., "Your room looks great! What a great job you did straightening up all those books and CDs!") rather than offering more general praise (e.g., "Thanks for cleaning your room.").

Thoughtful/Mindful Parenting

The general idea is to think about what your teen is learning from a given situation or interaction. Consider a variety of situations, both anxiety-related and routine. What behaviors are you reinforcing? Is your teen getting rewarded for behaviors you want to continue? Or for behaviors you want to stop?

Also, think about what your own behavior is modeling for your teen. Ask yourself "What did my teen just learn from that interaction/situation?" or "What message am I sending to my teen?"

Parent Handout #3
Parenting Anxious Teens

Limit-setting

Parents often have difficulty setting limits with their anxious teen. It seems counterintuitive to punish or threaten punishment for a teen who is clearly anxious and distressed. While you might handle a teen who is refusing to go to school because she simply does not want to go differently from a teen who is refusing to go to school because she is anxious, the end result should still be the same—the child must go to school. Also, parents tend to tolerate behaviors from their anxious teen (yelling, whining, even cursing) that they would not tolerate in other settings, thinking that the teen's obvious distress makes that behavior "okay." But the lack of negative consequences, combined with often being allowed to avoid the anxious situation, reinforces both the bad behavior and the avoidance. Rules are rules, and no one in the family should be able to get away with bad behavior without consequences.

Also, although our emotions may not be completely under our control, our behaviors are. We have all had moments when we have been so angry at others we've wanted to yell, scream, or even strike out at them, but we did not do any of those things because those behaviors are not appropriate. Similarly, your teen must learn that feeling anxious does not give her the right to act inappropriately. She may be very upset; she may feel anxious and angry and frustrated all at once. But she still needs to obey house rules, and she needs to be able to calm herself. This is a valuable life skill for her to develop, for although this program is designed to treat her panic disorder, she will certainly experience anxiety throughout her life, and she must be able to cope with that anxiety appropriately.

Allowing Natural Consequences (or How Not to Enable Your Teen's Anxiety)

One way to get out of the trap of feeling like the bad guy is to allow the natural consequences of your teen's anxiety, rather than helping her negotiate around those consequences. For example, parents often drive their teen to school because otherwise her anxiety in the morning will cause her to be late. Typically, the school has consequences for being late (e.g., detention, demerits, etc.) that are in place to help teens learn to be on time. By helping her avoid the consequence, you are reinforcing (a) that she needs or deserves special accommodations because of her anxiety and (b) that she can put off going to school in the morning because you will make sure she gets there on time.

Expecting/Anticipating Anxiety and Anxious Situations

As described in the handout "Parenting Anxious Youth: 101," parents often become so accustomed to their teen's anxiety that they anticipate it for her. For example, pulling the teen out of potentially anxiety-provoking situations in advance or asking questions repeatedly before an event (e.g., "Are you sure you're okay with this? Do you think you can do this?") or during an event ("Are you holding up okay? How are you? Do you need me to do anything?") signal to the teen that she is not capable of handling the situation. Also, asking repeatedly how the teen is feeling will cause her to hyperfocus on her physical sensations; this level of attention given to feelings can often increase the likelihood of panic.

Instead of focusing on your teen's anxiety, you should be indicating to her that she is completely capable of coping with the situation and that her anxiety is natural and harmless. Do this by expecting that she will attend family functions/outings (e.g., "Remember, we've got Aunt Sue's BBQ this weekend."), offering occasional words of encouragement (e.g., "You're doing so great!"), focusing on the positive (e.g., "This is such a fun BBQ!"), and generally letting her have the space needed to experience and enjoy the situation.

Parent Handout #4
What To Do (and Not To Do) in the Face of Panic

Now that your teen is engaging in various exposures and no longer avoiding situations that make him feel anxious, you may actually notice an increase (for a short time) in the number of panic attacks that he has. It is important, therefore, that you know how to handle a panic attack (or a potential panic attack).

Panic attacks not only feel scary to the person experiencing them, they often look scary to other people. When your teen is in the midst of a panic attack, he may cry, scream, shake, hyperventilate, and say things such as "I think I'm dying!" or "I'm losing it!" or "I think I'm going to faint!" Being in close proximity to such high levels of emotion is enough to make anyone feel anxious or worked up, but for parents to witness such emotion in their own child can be heartbreaking. As stated earlier, one of the most basic parental instincts is to protect your child, so when your teen gets upset, you want to jump in and fix things. However, as you have learned by now, while panic feels (and looks) scary, it is, in fact, *harmless*. So, while you may want to calm your child down because he looks so distressed, some of the ways in which you may interact with your teen during panic attacks can inadvertently make the situation worse.

Downward Spiral of Panic #1: Mimicking Your Teen's Panic

The teen starts to panic. (*Oh my God, I can't breathe!*) →

The parent gets upset and responds with strong emotion. (*What do you mean you can't breathe? You need to sit down, you're white as a sheet!*) →

The teen, feeding on the parent's alarmed reaction, continues to panic. (*I don't feel right—my heart is pounding, my chest hurts, I can't breathe!!*) →

The parent, getting more frightened, becomes frantic. (*We need to get you out of the store! Maybe we should call the doctor!*) →

The teen, seeing how scared and upset the parent is, becomes even more frightened, and the panic increases. (*The doctor?!? Oh my God, I'm dying, aren't I! I'm having a heart attack!*) →

This cycle of upset continues until the panic attack naturally subsides.

Downward Spiral of Panic #2: Desperately Seeking Calm

The teen starts to panic. (*Oh my God, I can't breathe!*) →

The parent gets upset and tries to calm the teen down. (*What's the matter? Are you hyperventilating? We need to find you a paper bag!*) →

The teen, responding to the parent's cue that hyperventilating is dangerous, continues to panic. (*No, really, I can't breathe! I do need a paper bag! I need to sit down!*) →

The parent starts frantically trying to get the teen to calm down. (*Just try breathing slowly, like this, in and out, in and out.*) →

The teen tries this, but because the panic has already escalated, cannot do so. (*I am trying, but I can't. I can't catch my breath! Something must be really wrong with me!!*) →

This cycle of upset continues until the panic attack naturally subsides.

Ideal Responses to Your Teen's Panic

Instead of participating in the downward spiral of panic, we recommend that you stay calm in the face of your teen's panic. Emphasize that he has the skills to handle the panic and that it is not dangerous. Be empathic—remind him that you know it is uncomfortable, but that it is short-lived and will be over soon. Sometimes, in the very early stages of a panic attack, teens might be able to calm themselves down and prevent a full attack from occurring. Once it has reached a critical point, however, there is just no way to stop the attack from coming, and they need to "ride the wave" of anxiety.

The Ideal #1: Prevented Panic

The teen starts to panic. (*Oh my God, I can't breathe!*) →

The parent remains calm and reassuring. (*You're starting to feel really anxious; that makes sense since this is the first time you've been to this mall in a long time. Try to use your skills to calm yourself down.*) →

The teen uses some cognitive restructuring and/or limited relaxation skills and is able to calm down and prevent the panic attack.

The Ideal #2: The Minimized Attack

The teen starts to panic. (*Oh my God, I can't breathe!*) →

The parent remains calm and reassuring. (*You're starting to feel really anxious; that makes sense since this is the first time you've been to this mall in a long time. Try to use your skills to calm yourself down.*) →

The teen tries to use the skills, but continues to panic. (*I've tried everything! I can't calm down; I need to get out of here!*) →

The parent remains calm, reminds the teen of what he already knows, and tries to focus on a post-panic reward. (*OK, so you might have a panic attack. I know you're uncomfortable, but you're not in any danger. We can't leave because, if we do, the panic wins. How about we go sit on that bench over there until it passes? Once it does, we can continue with our quest for the perfect pair of back-to-school shoes.*) →

The teen does have a panic attack, but is able to put it in perspective afterwards. (*That wasn't as bad as some other ones. I was able to remember that it wouldn't last forever and that I wasn't going to die.*)

Remember that with thoughtful/mindful parenting, you want to consider what message your actions/behaviors send to your teen. If you get frantic, look scared, or desperately try to get your teen to calm down, you further the notion that panic is bad or dangerous and must be stopped immediately. If you remain calm, however, you send the signal that your teen is going to be fine, whether or not he actually panics.

Parent Handout #5
You and Your Less Anxious Teen

Like most parents, you likely came to therapy thinking, "I just want my teen to feel better. I want her to be like a normal teenager, and not feel so anxious all the time." Be careful what you wish for!

On Having a Normal Teenager

Normal teenagers fight with their parents. Normal teenagers break rules and test limits. Their job, as teenagers, is to figure out who they are, and they can only do that if they differentiate themselves (to varying degrees) from their families. While you may have thought you wanted a normal teenager, after the tenth time you've had to drop your teen at the mall in one week or the umpteenth fight you have over whether or not she can skip a family function to go out with friends, you may begin to wish you had that anxious teen back again—the one who didn't want to go anywhere without you and preferred being at home to anywhere else in the world.

Mourning the Loss

It is okay for you to feel some sadness and regret over the distance that may develop as your teen begins to have a more independent life. However, it is important to remember that this is an important stage in your teen's development. Picture your teen as an adult—what are the things you want for her? A happy relationship? A good job? A family? These come from figuring out who she is and becoming an independent adult. It is your teen's job to fight with you and separate somewhat from you; it does not mean that you are "losing" her, it just means that she is developing. And that's a good thing!

Find New Ways to Bond with Your Teen

Now that your teen is starting to do things on her own, you may feel that panic is no longer the "glue" keeping your relationship feeling close and together. So, if you are no longer needed to help your teen through panic attacks because your teen already has these skills, it is important that you and your teen find new ways to bond and find time together. Once the panic attacks decrease, you may begin to feel as if you are not needed anymore, but that is not true. We know that building a good relationship with your teen now will help her navigate the teenage years and beyond. So, focus on finding new, positive things you can do together regularly that don't involve panic, such as going out to lunch together, shopping together, going to a concert or sporting event together, and the like. Brainstorm with your teen fun activities that you and she can do together. Now that panic is not ruling your teen's life anymore, you are free to enjoy so many more things together! Enjoy this opportunity!!!

Adjusting the Volume, Not Changing the Station

Some parents may find that, although their teen is no longer panicking (or avoiding feared situations), she is still more clingy than her siblings and still gets more anxious in certain situations than other teens. While therapy does many things, it is not going to change who your child is at heart. Some people are introverts, others are extroverts, and still others are somewhere in between. None of these is good or bad, and the world would be a boring place if everyone were the same. If you think of your teen as a radio, therapy is not going to change the station, it just adjusts the volume. In other words, therapy helps turn the anxiety volume down to a manageable, acceptable level; it does not turn your child into an entirely different person, nor would we want to do so! Teens who are temperamentally more anxious are often sensitive, empathic, and caring. Be sure to focus on the positive qualities your child possesses—there are plenty of them!

References

Alessi, N. E., Robbins, D. R., & Dilsaver, S. C. (1987). Panic and depressive disorders among psychiatrically hospitalized adolescents. *Psychiatry Research, 20,* 275–283.

American Psychiatric Association. (1994). *The diagnostic and statistical manual of mental disorders* (4th ed.). Washington, D. C.: American Psychiatric Association.

Antony, M. M. (2005). Five strategies for bridging the gap between research and clinical practice. *Behavior Therapist, 28,* 162–163.

Barlow, D. H., Craske, M. G., Cerney, J. A., & Klosko, J. S. (1989). Behavioral treatment of panic disorder. *Behavior Therapy, 20,* 261–282.

Barlow, D. H., Gorman, J. M., Shear, M. K., & Woods, S. W. (2000). Cognitive-behavioral therapy, imipramine, or their combination for panic disorder: A randomized controlled trial. *Journal of the American Medical Association, 283,* 2529–2536.

Barlow, D. H., & Seidner, A. L. (1983). Treatment of adolescent agoraphobics: Effects on parent-adolescent relations. *Behaviour Research and Therapy, 21,* 519–526.

Barrios, B.A., & O'Dell, S.L. (1989). Fears and anxieties. In: E.J. Mash & R.A. Barkley (Eds.), *Treatment of Childhood Disorders.* New York: Guilford Press.

Biederman, J., Faraone, S. V., Marrs, A., Moore, P., Barcia, J., Ablon, S., et al. (1997). Panic disorder and agoraphobia in consecutively referred children and adolescents. *The Journal of the American Academy of Child and Adolescent Psychiatry, 36,* 214–223.

Birmaher, B., Ryan, N. D., & Williamson, D. E. (1996). Depression in children and adolescents: Clinical features and pathogenesis. In K. I. Shulman, M. Tohen, & S. P. Kutcher (Eds.), *Mood disorders across the life span* (pp. 51–81). New York: Wiley-Liss.

Braswell, L. (1991). Involving parents in cognitive behavioral therapy with children and adolescents. In: P.C. Kendall (Ed.), *Child and Adolescent Therapy.* New York: Guildford Press.

Brown, T. A., DiNardo, P. A., & Barlow, D. H. (1994). *Anxiety Disorders Interview Schedule for DSM-IV (ADIS-IV)*. San Antonio, TX: Psychological Corporation.

Craske, M. G., & Barlow, D. H. (2006). *Mastery of your anxiety and panic: Therapist guide* (4th ed.). New York: Oxford University Press.

Dadds, M.R., Heard, P.M., & Rapee, R.M. (1992). The role of family intervention in the treatment of child anxiety disorders: Some preliminary findings. *Behaviour Change, 9*, 171–177.

Diler, R. S., Birmaher, B., & Brent, D. A. (2004). Phenomenology of panic disorder in youth. *Depression and Anxiety, 20*, 39–43.

Essau, C. A., Conradt, J., & Petermann, F. (1999). Prevalence, comorbidity and psychosocial impairment of somatoform disorders in adolescents. *Health & Medicine, 4*, 169–180.

Fleming, J. E., Offord, D. R., & Boyle, M. H. (1989). Prevalence of childhood and adolescent depression in the community: Ontario child health study. *British Journal of Psychiatry, 155*, 647–654.

Ginsburg, G. S., Silverman, W. K., & Kurtines, W. M. (1995). Family involvement in treating children with phobic and anxiety disorders: A look ahead. *Clinical Psychology Review, 15*, 457–473.

Gotlib, I. H., Lewinsohn, P. M., & Seeley, J. R. (1998). Consequences of depression during adolescence: Marital status and marital functioning in early adulthood. *Journal of Abnormal Psychology, 107*, 686–690.

Hayward, C., Killen, J. D., & Kraemer, H. C. (1997). Assessment and phenomenology of nonclinical panic attacks in adolescent girls. *Journal of Anxiety Disorders, 11*, 17–32.

Hayward, C., Killen, J. D., & Kraemer, H. C. (2000). Predictors of panic attacks in adolescents. *Journal of the American Academy of Child & Adolescent Psychiatry, 39*, 207–214.

Heinrichs, N., Spiegel, D. A., & Hofmann, S. G. (2002). Panic disorder with agoraphobia. In F. W. Bond & W. Dryden (Eds.), *Handbook of brief cognitive behaviour therapy* (pp. 55–76). London: Wiley.

Hoffman, E. C., & Mattis, S. G. (2000). A developmental adaptation of panic control treatment for panic disorder in adolescence. *Cognitive and Behavioral Practice, 7*, 253–261.

Kearney, C. A., Albano, A. M., Eisen, A. R., Allan W. D., & Barlow, D. H. (1997). The phenomenology of panic disorder in youngsters: An empirical study of a clinical sample. *Journal of Anxiety Disorders, 11*, 49–62.

Keller, M. B., Yonkers, K. A., & Warshaw, M. G. (1994). Remission and relapse in subjects with panic disorder and panic with agoraphobia: A prospective short interval naturalistic follow-up. *Journal of Nervous and Mental Disease, 182*, 290–296.

King, N. J., Gullone, E., Tonge, B. J., & Ollendick, T. H. (1993). Self-reports of panic attacks and manifest anxiety in adolescents. *Behaviour Research and Therapy, 31,* 111–116.

King, N. J., Ollendick, T. H., Mattis, S. G., Yang, B., & Tonge, B. (1996). Nonclinical panic attacks in adolescents: Prevalence, symptomatology, and associated features. *Behaviour Change, 13,* 171–183.

Last, C. G., & Strauss, C. C. (1989). Panic disorder in children and adolescents. *Journal of Anxiety Disorders, 3,* 87–95.

Lewinsohn, P. M., Hops, H., Roberts, R. E., Seeley, J. R., & Andrews, J. A. (1993). Adolescent psychopathology: I. Prevalence and incidence of depression and other DSM-III-R disorders in high school students. *Journal of Abnormal Psychology, 102,* 133–144.

Macaulay, J. L., & Kleinknecht, R. A. (1989). Panic and panic attacks in adolescents. *Journal of Anxiety Disorders, 3,* 221–241.

Masi, G., Favilla, L, Mucci, M., & Millepiedi, S. (2000). Panic disorder in clinically referred children and adolescents. *Child Psychiatry and Human Development, 31,* 139–151.

Mattis, S. G., Pincus, D. B., Ehrenreich, J. T., & Barlow, D. H. (2007). *Treatment of panic disorder in adolescence: Results from a randomized clinical trial.* Unpublished manuscript (currently under review for publication), Boston University.

Moreau, D. L., & Follet, C. (1993). Panic disorder in children and adolescents. *Child and Adolescent Psychiatric Clinics of North America, 2,* 581–602.

Ollendick, T. H. (1995). Cognitive behavioral treatment of panic disorder with agoraphobia in adolescents: A multiple baseline design analysis. *Behavior Therapy, 26,* 517–531.

Ollendick, T.H., & King, N.J. (1998). Empirically supported treatments for children with phobic and anxiety disorders: Current status. *Journal of Clinical Child Psychology, 27,* 156–167.

Ost, L., Westling, B. E., & Hellstrom, K. (1994). Applied relaxation, exposure in vivo and cognitive methods in the treatment of panic disorder with agoraphobia. *Behavior Research and Therapy, 31,* 383–394.

Pine, D. S., Cohen, P., Gurley, D., Brook, J., & Ma, Y. (1998). The risk for early-adulthood anxiety and depressive disorder in adolescents with anxiety and depressive disorders. *Archives of General Psychiatry, 55,* 56–64.

Shear, M. K., Brown, T. A., Barlow, D. H., Money, R., Sholomskas, D. E., Woods, S. W., et al. (1997). Multicenter collaborative panic disorder severity scale. *American Journal of Psychiatry, 154,* 1571–1575.

Silverman, W. K., & Albano, A. M. (1997). *Anxiety Disorders Interview Schedule for DSM-IV, Child & Parent Versions.* San Antonio, TX: Psychological Corporations.

Silverman, W. K., Fleisig, W., Rabian, B., & Peterson, R. A. (1991). Childhood Anxiety Sensitivity Index. *Journal of Clinical Child Psychology, 20,* 162–168.

Thyer, B. A., Parrish, R. T., Curtis, G. C., Nesse, R. M., & Cameron, O. G. (1985). Ages of onset of DSM-III anxiety disorders. *Comparative Psychiatry, 26,* 113–122.

Weissman, M. M., Wolk, S., Goldstein, R. B., Moreau, D., Adams, P., Greenwald, S., et al. (1999). Depressed adolescents grown up. *Journal of the American Medical Association, 281,* 1707–1713.

Wittchen, H., Reed, V., & Kessler, R. C. (1998). The relationship of agoraphobia and panic in a community sample of adolescents and young adults. *Archives of General Psychiatry, 55,* 1017–1024.

Yonkers, K. A., Zlotnick, C., Allsoworth, J., Warshaw, M., Shea, T., & Keller, M. B. (1998). Is the course of panic disorder the same in women and men? *American Journal of Psychiatry, 155,* 596–602.

About the Authors

Donna B. Pincus is an Associate Professor and is also the Director of the Child and Adolescent Fear and Anxiety Treatment Program at the Center for Anxiety and Related Disorders at Boston University. Dr. Pincus received her Ph.D. in clinical psychology from Binghamton University in 1999, after completing an internship at the University of Florida Health Sciences Center, with a child/pediatric specialty. Dr. Pincus has focused her clinical research career on the development of new treatments for child anxiety disorders. Dr. Pincus is the principal investigator of several research grants from the National Institute of Mental Health that focus on developing new treatments for early childhood separation anxiety disorder and adolescent panic disorder. She has published numerous articles and chapters on the assessment and treatment of child and adolescent anxiety disorders. In addition to her involvement with research, she trains and mentors doctoral students at Boston University and treats children and adults with anxiety disorders with cognitive-behavioral therapy. Dr. Pincus is also the Editor and creator of The Child Anxiety Network (*www.childanxiety.net*), an online resource for parents, teachers, psychologists and other professionals who want accurate information and resources on child anxiety. She has given numerous workshops on child anxiety to parents, teachers, students, and healthcare professionals, and her work with children and adolescents with anxiety disorders have been featured on both local and national media networks, including Good Morning America, ABC News' 20–20 Downtown, Women's Lifetime Television, and NBC's Today Show.

Jill T. Ehrenreich received her Ph.D. from the University of Mississippi in 2002, following an internship in the Department of Child and Adolescent Psychiatry at the University of Chicago, and has published several articles and chapters in the area of child and adolescent anxiety disorders. She has also written parent and adolescent workbooks and a therapist guide that utilize a unified treatment approach for adolescents with anxiety and mood disorders, which employs both cognitive-behavioral and emotion-focused techniques. In her current roles as Director of the Youth Emotional Disorders Research Program, Center for Anxiety and Related Disorders (CARD) and Assistant Research Professor, Department of Psychology, Boston University, she maintains an active program of research exploring the etiology, assessment, and treatment of child and adolescent anxiety and related disorders, with a particular focus on emotion and parenting influences. In this capacity, she also co-mentors a team of doctoral students in their clinical research training and supervises their provision of cognitive-behavioral treatment services to child and adolescents at CARD. She serves on the Editorial Boards of *The Behavior Therapist* and *Journal of Anxiety Disorders* and is currently the Leader of the Child and Adolescent Anxiety Special Interest Group within the Association of Behavioral and Cognitive Therapies.

Sara G. Mattis received her Ph.D. from Virginia Polytechnic Institute and State University in 1997 after completing her internship at Boston Children's Hospital and Judge Baker Children's Center, Harvard Medical School. She has published several journal articles and book chapters on childhood anxiety, and is the co-author of *Panic Disorder and Anxiety in Adolescence* (2002). Dr. Mattis has served as Director of the Child and Adolescent Fear and Anxiety Treatment Program as well as Director of the Adolescent Panic Treatment Program at the Center for Anxiety and Related Disorders (CARD) at Boston University. She is currently a consultant with the Child and Adolescent Program at CARD. Dr. Mattis has a private practice in Winchester, MA where she specializes in the treatment of anxiety disorders in children, adolescents, and adults.